History of India and Indian Mythology

An Enthralling Guide to Major Civilizations, Empires, Events, People, and Myths

© Copyright 2023 - All rights reserved.

The content contained within this book may not be reproduced, duplicated, or transmitted without direct written permission from the author or the publisher.

Under no circumstances will any blame or legal responsibility be held against the publisher, or author, for any damages, reparation, or monetary loss due to the information contained within this book, either directly or indirectly.

Legal Notice:

This book is copyright protected. It is only for personal use. You cannot amend, distribute, sell, use, quote, or paraphrase any part, or the content within this book, without the consent of the author or publisher.

Disclaimer Notice:

Please note the information contained within this document is for educational and entertainment purposes only. All effort has been executed to present accurate, up-to-date, reliable, and complete information. No warranties of any kind are declared or implied. Readers acknowledge that the author is not engaging in the rendering of legal, financial, medical, or professional advice. The content within this book has been derived from various sources. Please consult a licensed professional before attempting any techniques outlined in this book.

By reading this document, the reader agrees that under no circumstances is the author responsible for any losses, direct or indirect, that are incurred as a result of the use of the information contained within this document, including, but not limited to, errors, omissions, or inaccuracies.

Free limited time bonus

Stop for a moment. We have a free bonus set up for you. The problem is this: we forget 90% of everything that we read after 7 days. Crazy fact, right? Here's the solution: we've created a printable, 1-page pdf summary for this book that you're reading now. All you have to do to get your free pdf summary is to go to the following website:

https://livetolearn.lpages.co/enthrallinghistory/

Once you do, it will be intuitive. Enjoy, and thank you!

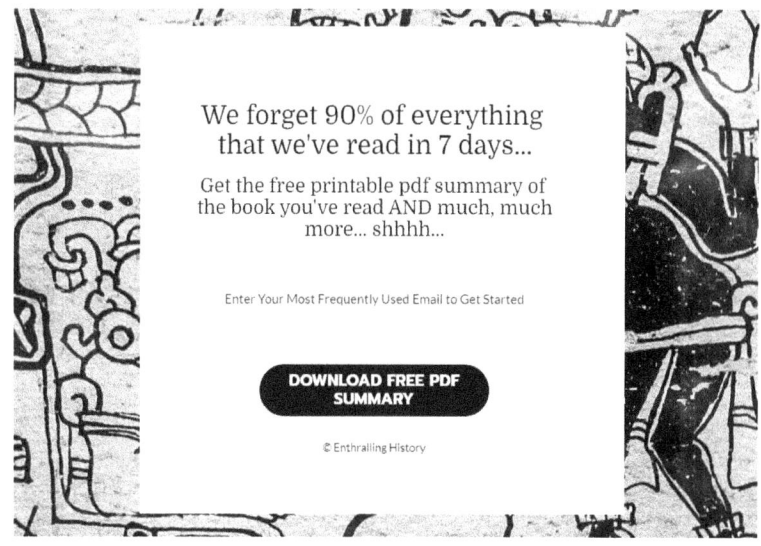

Table of Contents

PART 1: HISTORY OF INDIA 1
    INTRODUCTION 2
    CHAPTER 1: INDIA: AN ANCIENT INTRODUCTION 4
    CHAPTER 2: THE INDUS VALLEY CIVILIZATION AND THE INDO-ARYANS 9
    CHAPTER 3: MEDIEVAL INDIA AND ITS EMPIRES (600-1450 CE) 21
    CHAPTER 4: THE MUGHAL EMPIRE: A STRUGGLE FOR SUPREMACY 31
    CHAPTER 5: COLONIAL INDIA AND THE EAST INDIA COMPANY 44
    CHAPTER 6: GANDHI: FREEDOM AND PARTITION 55
    CHAPTER 7: THE INDIAN REPUBLIC 61
    CHAPTER 8: INDIAN CULTURE 69
    CHAPTER 9: INFLUENTIAL INDIANS IN HISTORY 75
    CHAPTER 10: BUDDHISM VS HINDUISM 81
    CONCLUSION 87
    DATES 89
    GLOSSARY 92

PART 2: INDIAN MYTHOLOGY 95
    INTRODUCTION 96
    CHAPTER 1: THE HINDU COSMOS 98
    CHAPTER 2: VISHNU AND HIS MANY AVATARS 107
    CHAPTER 3: SHIVA THE DESTROYER 120
    CHAPTER 4: HINDU GODDESSES PART I 131

- CHAPTER 5: HINDU GODDESSES PART II 142
- CHAPTER 6: KRISHNA THE SUPREME 153
- CHAPTER 7: GANESHA, LORD OF LUCK 161
- CHAPTER 8: TALES FROM THE *MAHABHARATA* 171
- CHAPTER 9: TALES FROM THE *RAMAYANA* 182
- CONCLUSION 192

HERE'S ANOTHER BOOK BY ENTHRALLING HISTORY THAT YOU MIGHT LIKE 194

FREE LIMITED TIME BONUS 195

BIBLIOGRAPHY 196

Part 1: History of India

An Enthralling Overview of Significant Civilizations, Empires, Events, People, and Religion

Introduction

The history of India is the history of an entire subcontinent. Today's India is a third the size of the US or Europe, but its history includes parts of what are now Pakistan, Bangladesh, and even Afghanistan. It also had a huge influence on other Asian countries, both directly in Cambodia and Srivijaya (today's Indonesia) and indirectly through the export of Buddhism to Southeast Asia, China, and Tibet.

India contained some of the earliest civilizations of the world and has an immensely rich history. India seems to have absorbed new influences rather than replacing the old; so, today, it contains a little of everything: rich Hindu culture, memories of the Mughals in architecture and art, British bureaucracy (try booking a ticket on Indian Railways!), tribal art, and a thriving new IT industry. Now a democratic and officially secular nation, India retains its incredible diversity.

All that richness can make Indian history confusing. So can the fact that until recently, much Indian history was seen through colonial eyes. The British Raj saw Indian history as the story of dynasties and tried to separate and distinguish different races; it assumed that India never changed ("essentialism" or "orientalism"). Often, only Sanskrit texts were used to understand Indian history, and the Islamic contribution to India was overlooked, as were medieval Hindu movements.

And true to their "divide and rule" strategy, the Raj historians saw Indian history as a succession of mutually exclusive eras. They didn't really understand how, for instance, a single king in southern India might sponsor Jain, Buddhist, and Hindu faiths without partiality or how emperor Akbar blended his wife's Rajput, Hindu heritage with his dynasty's Turkic, Muslim roots.

Different ages overlap. India today contains First Peoples living in the Andaman Islands, tribal peoples such as the Gond and Munda, workers in call centers and IT companies, shoeshine men, and bicycle rickshaw drivers. You may meet a US tech company's CEO climbing a holy mountain barefoot or a traditional painter who quit her job in marketing to join the family art studio.

But the overlapping of different layers doesn't make India eternal. The early collection of religious poetry called the Vedic corpus, or Vedas, hasn't changed since a millennium before the Common Era, but the way the texts have been interpreted and used certainly has. This book will show you how religion developed over the ages and sometimes distinctly in different areas of India.

This book will help you navigate the different streams of Indian history without getting swamped. First, it takes a broadly chronological approach; then, at the end, there is the chance to look more at personalities, Indian culture, and India today.

Some earlier histories are based on the work of the 19th and early 20th centuries, which was affected by colonialism even where the individual historian had no ax to grind. This book uses work from writers like Shashi Tharoor, who has analyzed the "benefits" of the empire in a slightly different way, as well as William Dalrymple, who has used Persian-language texts to reinterpret Mughal history and the early days of the British in India.

It's a big ask to cram thousands of years of history into a small book. But if you want to learn about Indian history without having to read, for instance, the 24 different volumes of the *New Cambridge History of India*, hopefully this book will give you a good start.

Chapter 1: India: An Ancient Introduction

To get started in Indian history, you must first understand the huge dimensions of the task. India is big, and it has a very, very long history.

Consider, for instance, that India today has the world's second-largest population (next to China) and is the seventh-largest country by geographical area. The 2011 census gave India 1.2 billion residents, and this grew to nearly 1.4 billion in 2022. (The US, by comparison, has a total population of 331 million.)

India is not only a very large but also a very diverse country. Its 1.3 million square miles include the high Himalayas, several deserts, rainforests, coasts on two oceans, and at least six different climate zones. Lambada, in the north, is on roughly the same latitude as North Africa; Kanyakumari, on the southern tip, is on the same latitude as Ethiopia, the Gambia, or Ecuador. It goes from sea level to the top of Kanchenjunga at 8,586 meters (28,170 feet)—the third-highest mountain in the world.

India is linguistically diverse, too, with twenty-two different officially recognized languages and many more unrecognized languages and dialects. About three-quarters of its languages come from the same Indo-Aryan family, with the unrelated Dravidian languages of South India (Tamil, Malayalam, Kannada, and Telegu) and two Sino-Tibetan languages (Manipuri and Bodo) making up most of the rest. Many Indians are multilingual, and educated Indians often speak Hindi, English, and at least one other Indian language.

In terms of religion, India is 80 percent Hindu and about 14 percent Muslim, with substantial Christian, Sikh, and Jain minorities. It also has a Buddhist minority that increased when 100,000 Tibetan refugees headed to India after the Chinese took over Tibet (the Dalai Lama was one of them) and with the mass conversion of nearly half a million Untouchables led by B.R. Ambedkar.

Identities can be very fluid. Ladakhi grandmothers wearing traditional long dresses and aprons share work in the fields with their Ray-Ban-wearing grandsons doing an MBA at IIT Delhi. A priest in a temple, wearing his formal robes and a trident mark on his forehead, might turn out to be a former cricket player or marketing manager. India is a place where a Christian girl from a scheduled tribe can become a boxing champion and a member of the Rajya Sabha (equivalent to a senate), and a low-caste ragpicker (garbage collector) can become the mayor of a big city.

The geography of India partly dictated its history. Its location between Central Asia to the northwest and China to the northeast meant that India was always open to influence, invasion, or commerce, but the Himalayas also formed a significant barrier so that India always stood slightly apart. Passes from Central Asia include the Swat Valley, the Hunza Valley, and the Khyber Pass—the latter becoming extremely important as Britain and Russia competed in the "Great Game" to dominate the area in the nineteenth century. On the west coast, maritime trade with East Africa, the Middle East, and (later) Portugal and England created wealth, while from the east coast, Indian influence reached Thailand, Cambodia, Burma, and Indonesia.

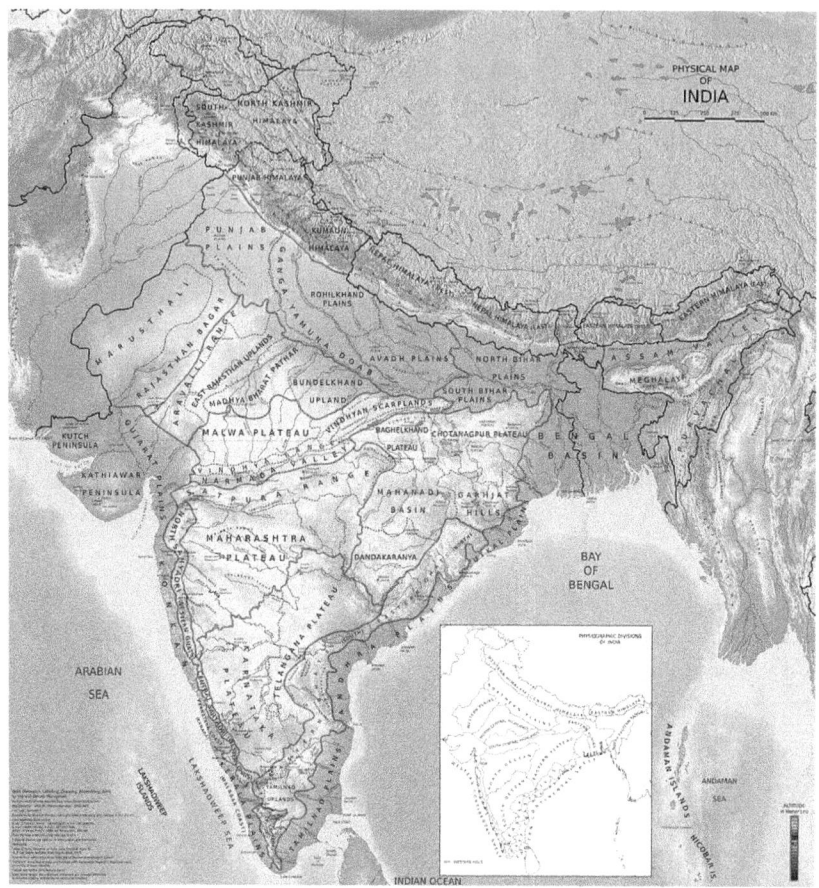

The map of India clearly shows the great Himalayan barrier to the north and the Indo-Gangetic Plain.
Vigneshdm1990, CC BY-SA 4.0 <https://creativecommons.org/licenses/by-sa/4.0>, via Wikimedia Commons; https://commons.wikimedia.org/wiki/File:Physical_Map_of_India.jpg

Within the subcontinent, regional differences are important, both geographically and culturally. India can be divided into three main regions: the north, from the Himalayas and the Hindu Kush down to the fertile Punjab (some of this area is now in Pakistan); the Gangetic plain of fertile silt, irrigated by the Ganges and Yamuna rivers; and the south, divided from the Gangetic plain by the Deccan Trap (an area of much-eroded volcanic basalt). Quite often, the history of each of these regions was different from that of others. For instance, while the Mughal Empire took over the north and the plains, it was never able to penetrate further south.

India's story began with a Paleolithic culture that used simple rock shelters. The most famous Stone Age site in India is Bhimbetka in central India, where over 750 rock shelters survive; cave paintings at Bhimbetka date from as early as 8,000 BCE. The earliest inhabitants of the site used basic stone tools such as flaked-off pebbles; later, in the Mesolithic period, they created new types of tools— microliths such as tiny arrowheads, which made hunting much easier. The paintings from this time depict themes of animals and hunting, as well as figures of pregnant women, showing a concern with fertility.

Mesolithic sites in other areas of northern and central India show that grain was being consumed since querns and rubbing stones for grinding flour have been found. Animal bones found at these sites include deer, boar, goat, and ostrich (the latter now extinct in India). Burials are often found inside the inhabited area, with grave goods; these people likely believed that the dead person's spirit would stay with them as part of the family, something that's found in other early cultures, such as Catal Huyuk in Turkey.

The Neolithic period saw a huge amount of progress. Agriculture became common, animals were domesticated, and pottery enabled better food storage; stone tools were now being highly polished, creating sharper edges and a striking improvement in efficiency. It's likely that small groups of Neolithic peoples overlapped across the country: remains have been found from this date in the Swat Valley and Kashmir and in the Godavari and Krishna valleys further south. Bhimbetka continued to be inhabited into historical times; later cave paintings show warriors on horseback or riding elephants.

While agriculture became advanced in the Chalcolithic period (2000-900 BCE), and the people of the ore-rich Aravalli Range developed metalworking in bronze and copper, these settlements don't appear to have developed into full-scale cities. It's likely the society of these settlements was relatively egalitarian, with a flat hierarchy and social structures based on clans. Many of these cultures would have still got a lot of their food from hunting or foraging, and agriculture may have been based at first on swidden cultivation—burning down an area of forest to use for a few years, then moving on once the soil was exhausted.

In later Indian texts, the forest becomes a scary place full of rakshasas (demons). For instance, in the Mahabharata, Krishna and Arjuna burn the Khandava forest totally to clear it for settlement. In the Ramayana, prince

Rama is exiled from the city of Ayodhya to the forest with his wife and brother. Even now, you may be told not to go into the "jungle" (a wild place) "because there are bad people there."

It's difficult to tell when exactly this happened, but as agriculture became widespread and populations became more settled, a polarity emerged between the village and the wilderness (grama / aranya) and the field and the forest (kshetra / vana) that resounds in later Indian culture. One guess would be that this may have happened around the time the first cities were created, which is the theme of the next chapter.

Chapter 2: The Indus Valley Civilization and the Indo-Aryans

The Indus Valley Civilization began in the northwest of the subcontinent, where the Indus and numerous other rivers flow through a wide and fertile alluvial plain. The area where this civilization grew is now divided between India and Pakistan, and the two major sites, Harappa and Mohenjo-daro, are both in Pakistan; however, the culture spread as far south as Rajasthan and Gujarat and east towards the Ganges. Traces of the culture have even been found as far west as Oman in the Persian Gulf, showing that these Indians traded extensively.

The Indus Valley Civilization appears to have begun around the beginning of the third millennium BCE or slightly earlier and lasted until 1750 BCE. Many sites show continuous occupation during this time, with substantial continuity of culture between the pre-Harappan, mature, and late periods. However, this culture disappeared completely from sight after its decline; the major sites were only discovered and excavated in the 1920s and 1930s.

These cities are extensive in scale and mark the beginning of urban culture in India. Mohenjo-daro covers 200 hectares, and the lower town there may have had a population of 42,000. Even if pre-Harappan sites don't show huge technological advances, evidently the system of social organization needed to be significantly more complex than that of the rock-shelter culture.

	Date
Pre-Harappan	Late 4th millennium BCE or earlier
Early Harappan	3300-2600
Mature period of Indus civilization	2600-1900 BCE
Late period of Indus civilization	1900-1750 BCE

Trade networks became quite extensive, linking different communities and leading to a uniform material culture across the different sites that have been found. Numerous crops were cultivated, including peas and cotton, and the water buffalo was domesticated. By the end of the early period, seals already used the Harappan script, which has still not been deciphered. (This may have been a pictorial script or even a counting method. Most of the inscriptions that have been found are very short—the longest is only 34 characters long, and most include only five or six signs—which makes it particularly difficult to interpret.)

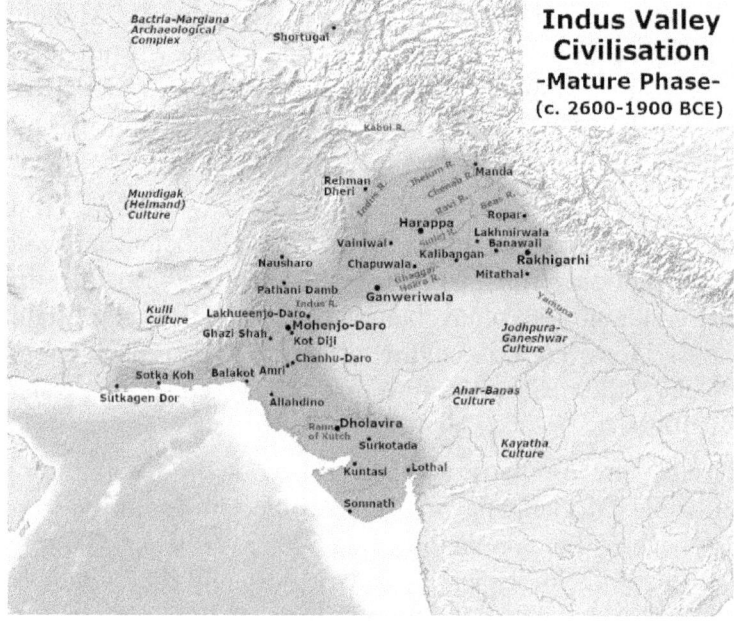

Map of the Indus Valley Civilization.

Avantiputra7, CC BY-SA 3.0 <https://creativecommons.org/licenses/by-sa/3.0>, via Wikimedia Commons; https://commons.wikimedia.org/wiki/File:Indus_Valley_Civilization,_Mature_Phase_(2600-1900_BCE).png

Indus Valley Civilization (IVC) cities had advanced town planning on a grid and a sanitation system, including the use of covered drains, as well as huge granaries allowing the inhabitants to store grain as insurance against drought. The massive walls of the cities may have been defensive but were also useful as protection against floods. Houses did not differ greatly in size or style, and almost all had access to wells for clean water; this gives the impression of a society without major extremes of wealth or poverty. Even in its ruined state, Mohenjo-daro is still very impressive.

Specialization of trades is already evident, with a concentration of particular trades in their own areas of the city. That's still the case in Indian towns today: all the candy makers are on one street, all the metalworkers on another.

The IVC had advanced metallurgy, including the use of lost-wax bronze casting and the use of copper, bronze, lead, tin, and various alloys, as well as gold. The IVC also developed a standardized system of weights and measures, and the use of a grid pattern for cities shows that the culture had some idea of surveying and geometry.

An intriguing feature of the IVC is that the cities appear not to have a sacred center. It seems likely, therefore, that religious ceremonies would have been carried out within the household. There are also no monumental tombs, as in other contemporary civilizations. One seal shows a seated figure with a horned headdress, surrounded by animals, which may be a sort of "horned god" figure, and female figurines may indicate a goddess cult, but archaeologists don't all agree with this interpretation.

The two greatest cities of the IVC, Harappa and Mohenjo-daro, flourished around 2600-2000 BCE. The cities then entered a decline and were eventually abandoned for reasons that remain unclear. It was earlier thought that an Aryan invasion destroyed the cities; however, it seems more likely that changes in the climate were responsible. The IVC had good drainage, but it did not have irrigation systems, which meant the cities were highly exposed to increases in temperature and changes in the course of rivers on which they depended. It seems likely that the people of the cities ended up making their way east towards the still-fertile Gangetic Plain.

Different cultures evolved elsewhere in India, but none were as spectacular as the Indus Valley culture. In the Indo-Gangetic Plain, iron was found by the first millennium BCE. Cut marks on bones show that cows were eaten; south of the Ganges, rice was cultivated, and terracotta animal figures are commonly found. There was a long continuity of small settlements, mainly of wattle and daub huts.

In the southern valleys of the Kaveri, Tungabhadra, Krishna, and Godavari rivers, small farming communities had emerged by the 3rd millennium BCE. They cultivated rice and millet and had sheep, goats, and buffalo. They buried their dead inside their huts—oddly, with their feet cut off.

By the first millennium, though, they had changed their burial rites and created megalithic sites for burial similar to those of non-Indian cultures. This was the time horses arrived in India, and harnesses are often found as grave goods together with hoes and sickles, as well as weapons. (Some later sites also include Roman coins, which shows how far Indian traders were voyaging.)

The Rig Veda and the Aryans

Around 1200 BCE is when India leaves prehistory and textual sources begin, including the Rig Veda and other Vedic texts. It is likely, though, that these texts were not written until considerably later but were transmitted orally for centuries. The main concern of these texts is to guide the reader in how to carry out religious rituals (a sort of instruction manual), so narrative is incidental and often has to be recreated from references that only hint at the myths.

In most areas, such as Europe or South and Central America, early cultures are known through their archeology but not through texts. In India, on the other hand, the early Aryan period is much better known through textual evidence, and there has been, until now, very limited archeological evidence.

Nineteenth and earlier 20th century historians believed that the Vedas were written by an Aryan people who had invaded from central Asia. However, the discovery of Harappan culture makes this theory unlikely. It seems more probable that there was a gradual migration of Aryan-language speakers and that existing Indian societies adapted (and adapted to) the newly arrived culture. It is intriguing that, though there is a linguistic link between the language of the Vedas and Old Iranian, gods and demons appear to have switched sides; the sun god Indra and the devas are "demons" in the Zend-Avesta (early Iranian scripture), while Ahura, a god in the Avesta, becomes the Indian Ashura, or demon.

Horse sacrifices are central in the Rig Veda as a means of proving the legitimacy of a ruler. Since no horses are known in the mid-Harappan, it seems likely that the new arrivals brought horses with them. On the other hand, it's quite notable that urban settlements, such as those at Mohenjo-daro and Harappa, are completely absent from the Rig Veda. It also doesn't mention exchange systems, so clearly the work was based on a very different form of society. (Rhinoceroses and tigers are shown on Harappan seals, but like towns, don't appear in the Rig Veda.)

Somewhat later than the Rig Veda, the two great epics Mahabharata (400 BCE) and Ramayana (500 BCE) were added, now written in pure Sanskrit. The Mahabharata tells the story of war set in the fertile plain around Delhi and likely recounts events that happened much earlier, perhaps around 950-800 BCE. In it, the Pandava brothers are set against the Kauravas, who have them exiled to the forest and later declare war on them. The Pandavas win with the help of Krishna, who gives one of them a philosophical lecture in the Bhagavad Gita (part of Book 6 of the Mahabharata). Krishna, a Yadava, is based in Dwarka, Gujarat, an area where the IVC still appears to have been active after the end of the Harappan cities.

As the action shifted from the Indus and Punjab to the Gangetic Plain, there was a gradual shift in the nature of agriculture and society. The Aryans were agro-pastoralists who used the cow as a measure of value and yokes of six or eight oxen to plow. They cultivated rice rather than wheat, which had been the staple of the north. They also came with new gods, the main deity being Agni, the god of fire, and worshiped them through sacrifices and other rituals. The hearth was the nucleus of worship in Aryan society. Other gods include the sun god Surya, Indra, Pushan, Savitri, and the death god Yama, as well as celestial beings like the Gandharvas.

(The word "Aryan" comes with a lot of baggage, having been used both by the British and later the Nazis to indicate a particular racial identity. We should really refer to them as "Aryan speakers." They appear to have been a linguistic community rather than a race and to have absorbed many of the existing communities in India over time.)

The Aryans appear to have brought with them the concept of a caste society, with four castes: the Brahmins or priests, the Kshatriya or rulers/warriors, the Vaishyas (farmers and merchants), and the Shudras (laborers). As mentioned, in the Veda, the concerns of the priests are primary; the reader is interested in how to perform rituals. However, by the time the Mahabharata was written, the Kshatriya clearly dominated; court politics, skirmishes, and fighting wars are its main subjects. The society that the Mahabharata describes is clearly very different from the flat society of the Indus Valley Civilization. The creation of the Shudra caste shows that labor has now become something that can be paid for, for instance.

In this regard, the practice of horse sacrifice is extremely important. A horse would have been an expensive investment, and the need for these costly sacrifices introduced a barrier to entry for clan chiefs and forced them to depend on the priests. This increased the status and power of the top two castes at the expense of the others.

Aryan religion is also based on the concepts of purity and pollution. Death, for instance, is a form of pollution; so is touching or eating and drinking with someone of an inferior caste. Aryan religion also introduced the idea of the cow as a sacred animal, with the result that cow dung and urine are considered pure in ritual terms. (Cow dung is actually used as a major source of fuel for both heating and cooking in traditional Indian life.)

This society must have looked a little like an early Celtic society, based on clans with chiefs who were involved in cattle raiding but also in extensive alliance-building through gift-giving. Genealogies started to become important at this time as temporary war leaders gave way to dynasties.

Re-emergence of Urban Culture

Around 600 BCE, towns began to re-emerge, mainly in the Ganges Basin, and tended to be located in the hills flanking the basin rather than on the plain itself. Commercial centers arose at Champa, Rajagriha, Kaushambi, Kashi (Varanasi), Vaishali, Shravasti, Ujjain, and Taxila. Around 500 BCE, Kaushambi appears to have had a population of around 36,000—a significantly-sized city. Wet rice cultivation in this area could yield three crops a year, creating a significant agricultural surplus that could support the population of the cities.

Towns such as Kaushambi, Rajagriha, and Shravasti covered large areas. They traded long-distance, particularly for luxury items, and coinage was introduced around this time. It is possible that the first coinage was the invention of market professionals, rather than rulers, aimed at meeting their needs for a more secure and simpler method of exchange than barter.

The change in social organization from a chieftain-led raiding culture to an urban culture of gana-sanghas (assemblies) created a new intellectual environment. Debate between competing ideologies and philosophies became common. At the same time, the number of castes went from four to two: Kshatriya, the ruling class, and dasa-karmakara, laborers and/or slaves. The language also changed from Sanskrit to Prakrit, which became the lingua franca of a large area of India.

New Hindu sects were started around this time, including the monastic Ajivikas and the materialist Charvakas. It was in this environment that two great religious leaders were born: Mahavira, founder of the Jain religion at Vaishali, and Shakyamuni Buddha in Kapilavastu. In many ways, their teachings were similar, including a stress on ahimsa, nonviolence. Some Jain ascetics even wear masks so they don't inadvertently breathe in gnats and other small creatures.

Both Buddha and Mahavira saw the goal of life as purification or enlightenment. Both created monastic communities of ascetics, perhaps drawing on urban culture for the idea of a custom-made community. Certainly, it would have been difficult to establish such monasteries without the existence of wealthy towns that could supply them with donations.

Buddha was born a prince of the Shakya clan, but having seen old age, sickness, and death, was shaken out of his comfortable lifestyle and spent years searching for truth until he finally achieved enlightenment. He evolved the doctrine of the Four Noble Truths: (1) all beings experience suffering, (2) suffering arises from desire and attachment, (3) liberation from attachment brings liberation from suffering, and (3) the eightfold path (symbolized by the eight-spoked wheel) can bring any human being to enlightenment.

Buddhism appears to have been initially a non-deistic philosophy. It also supported social freedom, refusing to recognize caste, and replaced the idea of divine kings with the theory of a social contract. Both Buddhists and Jains, in fact, made the two top castes useless: priests were not needed since sacrificial rites were not required, and warriors would have to rethink their status to suit the new ethic of nonviolence.

The Maurya Empire

The next major change in Indian history came in the fourth century BCE with the creation of the Maurya Empire. Chandragupta Maurya, the first emperor, took over the Magadha state, which had expanded to cover most of the Ganges Basin. He then expanded his lands towards the Indus in the north, where Alexander the Great had left a power vacuum behind after an inconclusive invasion. He took Persian territories in Afghanistan and Baluchistan, including Gandhara, where a Buddhist style of art that reflected the Hellenistic art of the time had evolved.

But Chandragupta doesn't appear to have been a diehard warrior. At the end of his career, he abdicated in favor of his son Bindusara and became a Jain ascetic.

Bindusara continued the expansion of his campaigns in the Deccan, but his son Ashoka brought the Mauryan Empire to its height. Ashoka is referred to as Chakravartin (world ruler) in Buddhist texts. He transformed the infrastructure of India, for instance building the Great North Road from Taxila (now in Pakistan) to Pataliputra (now Patna). This route was the Great Trunk Road of the British Raj and then National Highway No. 1 until 2010; it has now been renumbered No. 3 and No. 44, running all the way from the Pakistan border to New Delhi.

Ashoka took the task of standardizing the law seriously and made inscriptions of his edicts in Brahmi script across his empire. (He also used Greek and Aramaic languages in some places since these languages were spoken across the Persian Empire and there were still many Greek communities in Ashoka's domains.) In the Ganges Plain, he used rock pillars; elsewhere, texts were inscribed directly onto rock faces. These edicts present the earliest writing that survives in India apart from the still-undeciphered Harappan script.

Shocked by the violence of his campaign against Kalinga in eastern India, Ashoka converted to Buddhism a few years later. Unlike many rulers of his time, he refers to his personal experiences in some of his inscriptions: "Directly, after the Kalingas had been annexed, began His Sacred Majesty's zealous protection of the Law of Piety, his love of that Law, and his inculcation of that Law. Thence arises the remorse of His Sacred Majesty for having conquered the Kalingas because the conquest of a country previously unconquered involves the slaughter, death, and carrying away captive of the people. That is a matter of profound sorrow and regret to His Sacred Majesty" (Smith, 185). Perhaps he inherited this element of his nature from his grandfather, though he adopted the Buddhist religion rather than Jain asceticism.

Ashoka's edicts endorse nonviolence, doing good deeds, and generosity. In some of the minor edicts, he refers to his conversion, although he supported other religious bodies, such as the Ajivikas and—like other emperors after him—aimed to create a pluralistic state in which all faiths were respected.

The Ashoka pillar at Vaishala.
Amaan Imam, CC BY-SA 4.0 <https://creativecommons.org/licenses/by-sa/4.0>, via Wikimedia Commons; https://commons.wikimedia.org/wiki/File:N-BR-39_Ashokan_Pillar_Vaishali_%282%29.jpg

Ashoka's capital at Pataliputra (Patna) was strategically positioned between northern India and the Indo-Gangetic Plain. To the south, he had friendly relations with the Cholas, Pandyas, and Keralaputras (Cheras). He had close links with Lanka, where his son Mahinda is said to have been a Buddhist missionary, and gifted it with a branch of the Bodhi Tree under which Buddha received enlightenment.

The Maurya Empire was a largely agrarian empire where the state controlled the irrigation system and used tax revenues to pay for it. Archeology shows that the empire had a high standard of living, with brick houses, stone palaces in Pataliputra, and highly polished stone sculptures. Ashoka planted trees along the roads for shelter from the sun and built watering places along the major routes. He created provincial administrations at Ujjain, Taxila, and Suvarnagiri (Kanakagiri) and maybe also at Girnar and Dhauli; around the periphery of his empire, though, people were still living in megalithic societies.

Ashoka created what has been seen as a golden age for India. However, his successors failed to keep his empire in good health. The ninth and last Mauryan ruler was replaced in a military coup by his general, Pushpamitra, founder of the Shunga dynasty, around 185 BCE. The Shunga continued to rule Magadha in the east of the Ganges Basin, while northern areas such as Punjab, Haryana, and Rajasthan returned to clan-based rule.

The absence of strong rulership in northern India allowed the Central Asian empire of the Kushans to occupy the country as far south as Sarnath and Varanasi. The Kushans established trade along the Silk Roads between China and what is now Uzbekistan and as far as Rome in the west. It was these new trade routes that helped spread Buddhism to China; later, the Chinese would export Buddhism to Japan and other Asian nations.

South India saw the beginnings of state formation later than the north. Towns such as Madurai, Uraiyur, and Karur became established, and dynasties such as the Chola established their rule over large areas around the third century BCE. Around the same time, the Sangam literary corpus was established. Written in Tamil, it is very different from northern literature. The majority of it focuses on romantic and erotic subjects, with only a small amount of epic verse.

Buddhism and Jainism had become highly influential by the second century BCE, when the Great Stupa at Sanchi was built, together with numerous monasteries; another stupa was erected at Bharhut. At first, a majority of donations for the structures came from small landowners, artisans, and guilds, as well as from monks and nuns. (Note that relics, which stupas were built to enclose, are incompatible with Brahman rules of purity.)

The Vedic religion did not have sacred buildings; it was based on sacrifice, and sacrificial sites were temporary. Thus, it appears to have been the two newer religions that introduced the concept of sacred architecture in India. Rock-cut chaitya halls and viharas (monasteries) imitated wooden designs to begin with (for instance, at Karla, an early site) and are often relatively small in scale. But they soon increased in both size and complexity. Sites such as Ellora and Ajanta represent a further development; at Ellora, Hindu, Jain, and Buddhist works are all found at the same site and was often paid for by the same patrons.

Buddhism was originally aniconic; Buddha was not shown as a figure but represented by signs of his status, such as a parasol, an empty seat, or a miniature stupa. For instance, there is a bell-shaped stupa with a wooden parasol above it at the end of the Karla chaitya hall whereas, in a modern Buddhist temple, a statue of the Buddha would be expected. As time passed, Buddha started to be represented in human form, and influences from Hinduism later introduced other beings, such as protective gods, bodhisattvas, and so on.

The Gupta Empire

The next great empire in India was that of the Guptas, founded by Chandragupta I (not to be confused with Chandragupta Maurya) in 319 CE. The Gupta Empire has often been regarded as a golden age. Unlike the Maurya Empire, it was not highly centralized but allowed most decisions to be made locally.

Chandragupta married a Lichchhavi princess of Vaishali and extended his rule as far west as Allahabad and as far north as Nepal. However, the empire did not extend much farther south than the Ganges. His son, Samudragupta, expanded the empire much further into the Deccan, as far south as Tamil Nadu, north to Rajasthan and Punjab, and east into Bengal. However, it seems likely that many of these territories simply paid him tribute and managed their own affairs. In other words, he had financial but not political control. This appears to have been an effective formula, as the Gupta Empire would last until 532 CE—more than two centuries.

The Guptas made land grants an important feature of their rule, restructuring agriculture by giving grants to encourage the conversion of wasteland. Such grants were given to individuals, as well as to monasteries, temples, and seats of learning, such as the Buddhist university of Nalanda, which at one point owned 200 villages. (Xuanzang, a Chinese monk who visited India from 629-645, studied at Nalanda and describes it as an earthly paradise, with pools filled with blue lotus flowers, dazzling flame-tree flowers, and groves of mango trees for shade. When he returned to China, he took numerous Sanskrit texts with him, making a huge contribution to the expansion of Buddhism in China. Much later, in the sixteenth century, novelist Wu Cheng'en adapted his experiences as Journey to the West, or Monkey. You may have seen the TV series or played the videogame.)

Land grants were inscribed on copper plates, a good number of which survived. Clearly, there was now a bureaucracy and complex legal structure in which written records were important. An intriguing feature of the land grant system is that it allowed small-scale peasant agriculture to coexist with large-scale land ownership and infrastructure projects, such as dams and stepwells (wells with staircases built for easy access to groundwater level).

Hinduism, perhaps at least partly motivated by the challenge from the two "reform" religions, had moved on from Vedic times. Agni and Surya, the most important gods of the earlier period, faded; Vishnu and Shiva replaced them as the major gods, with shakti, or goddess cults, also emerging. Unlike the Vedic religion, which appears to have had no images of the gods, Hinduism now represented the god by an idol, lingam (phallic symbol), or rock. Animal sacrifices were now being replaced by puja, which involved giving grain or other vegetables to the deity, and darshan, viewing the sacred image, which is often hidden behind a gate or curtain that is opened to allow the worshiper to see the god.

However, the word "Hinduism" at this date is something of a misnomer since worshipers would have identified themselves as Vaishnava (worshiping Vishnu), Shaiva (worshiping Shiva), or Pashupata (another form of Shiva worship). The label "Hindu" arrived much later—in fact, with the Islamic invasions.

Nonetheless, the cults of different gods appear to have coexisted without problems, perhaps because they shared common philosophies and a common social structure.

Chapter 3: Medieval India and Its Empires (600-1450 CE)

Over nearly ten centuries, many civilizations and kingdoms came and went in India, and India also exported its culture elsewhere. For instance, the Mon kingdom (predecessor of Thailand) became Buddhist, though many Hindu rites were also built into the Thai form of Buddhism. Hindu rites such as the Royal Plowing Ceremony are particularly important to the Thai royal family, perhaps reflecting the way the horse sacrifice was used to legitimize Aryan kings. The Khmer Empire of the ninth to fifteenth centuries and the Srivijaya (Indonesian) empire of the seventh to twelfth centuries also incorporated both Hinduism and Buddhism.

China and Tibet also became Buddhist, and Chinese Buddhism reached Korea and then Japan just before 600 CE. However, China did not integrate Indian culture in the same way as the Southeast Asian countries, likely because it already had a highly developed imperial culture.

By this date, India was a highly sophisticated society that had already seen two major empires and had advanced scientific knowledge. For instance, before 499, the mathematician Aryabhata had calculated pi to four decimal places and understood how the earth rotated on its axis and how lunar eclipses occurred. Arab scholars, who had access to both ancient Greek and Indian mathematics, thought the Indians were more interesting and accomplished than the Greeks.

Southern India in the Middle Ages

A significant change during the medieval period was the emergence of the south and the Deccan compared to the dominance of northern India and the Indo-Gangetic Plain in earlier periods. Though dynasties came and went, in most cases, the rulers of different areas appear to have been evenly matched. So, despite tensions and occasional wars, no conclusive victory created a new empire with anything like the reach of the Maurya or Gupta empires.

In Tamil Nadu, there were two main dynasties: the Pandyas in Madurai ruling the south and the Palas, or Pallavas, in Kanchipuram ruling the north. The second Pallava emperor, Mahendravarman I (ruled c. 600-630), was a musician, poet, painter, and scholar; he was also responsible for creating the earliest temples in Mamallapuram, which were cut out of rock. Unlike earlier rock-cut architecture, though, the rock was cut down on each side to leave the temples freestanding.

During Mahendravarman's rule, wars with the Chalukya dynasty, which ruled in Badami, Karnataka, began; they continued under his son, Narasimhavarman. The balance swung back and forth, with each side reaching the other's capital at one point but unable to hold it.

A rock-cut temple at Mamallapuram with a rock-cut elephant.
© Vyacheslav Argenberg / http://www.vascoplanet.com/, CC BY 4.0
<https://creativecommons.org/licenses/by/4.0>, via Wikimedia Commons;
https://commons.wikimedia.org/wiki/File:Mahabalipuram,_Pancha_Rathas_2,_India.jpg

The Chalukyas were ruling at Badami by 543 when Pulakeshin I made a cliff inscription; he used both Sanskrit and the Kannada language. The Chalukyas continued to rule the Deccan Plateau for over 600 years, though their fortunes waxed and waned over the years. They were particularly important in developing the southern style of temple architecture, building temples at Badami, Aihole, and Pattadakal. The earliest temples at Badami were rock-cut, but later temples had finely made perforated screens on the windows, spires over the central shrine, and a pillared mandapa hall in front of the sanctuary.

Meanwhile, the southwestern kingdom of Kerala was ruled by the Chera Perumal dynasty. Kerala always seems to have remained slightly apart from the other kingdoms, though that never stopped the Pandyas from attempting to slice off parts of central Kerala for themselves.

The Rashtrakuta were a small clan that served the Chalukyas for many years. But in 753, Dantidurga Rashtrakuta turned against the Chalukyas and defeated them. He allied his new kingdom with the Pallavas, helping Nandivarman II regain his capital Kanchipuram from the Chalukyas, who had taken it. Nandivarman then married Dantidurga's daughter, linking the two dynasties. At their height around 850 to 900, the Rashtrakutas ruled most of India south of the Ganges and controlled the western seaboard and trade with Arabia. Dantidurga's successor Krishna I built the immense rock-cut Kailash temple at Ellora; this was an immensely wealthy and ambitious house.

However, the Rashtrakutas didn't have the staying power of the Chalukyas. From 972 onward, Rashtrakuta power declined, and by the end of the century, the Chalukyas had made a comeback. (The last Rashtrakuta emperor, Indra IV, became a Jain ascetic and took the vow of Sallekhana, gradually starving himself to death.)

These southern states mixed a number of different types of land tenure. Villages might pay tax on the land that they cultivated; some villages were donated to an individual or group or to a temple. Temple villages became more important as time went on. They also typically mixed different religions, though Buddhism gradually began to weaken, and royal patronage shifted towards Hindu and Jain foundations. At Badami, there are both Jain and Hindu rock-cut temples, and even though the Pallavas were Hindu, they sponsored a number of Jain temples, for example in Kanchipuram and Chitharal.

This period also saw the creation of the matha or mutt, a Hindu version of the Buddhist or Jain monastic community.

A large number of hero stones from the south have survived, most of them dating from 300 to about 1200. They commemorate the death of a hero in battle and are generally divided into a number of panels showing battle scenes, the hero worshiping a deity, and the hero in a palanquin or riding his horse. These stones may have served as the focus of a local cult.

Around 907, the Cholas, whose state was based around the Kaveri River, vastly increased their power. By the time of Rajaraja I (reigned 985-1014), the Cholas controlled most of Tamil Nadu, Kerala, and part of Karnataka, as well as northern Sri Lanka. Rajaraja built Thanjavur/Tanjore's "Big Temple" (the Brihadisvara or Rajarajesvarem Temple), which is considered one of the greatest of all the temples built in the southern style, with its 217-foot-high vimana tower. The Cholas supported Shaivism, giving their patronage to the temple of the dancing Shiva (Shiva Nataraja) at Chidambaram. By the late twelfth century, though, both the Cholas and the Chalukyas started to weaken, and things seem to have fallen apart quickly.

In the final centuries of the medieval period in India, two new dynasties, the Hoysala and Kakatiya, rose on the west coast in Karnataka. By 1245, the Hoysalas had taken over the Chola kingdom and most of the Pandyas' lands in southern Tamil Nadu. The Hoysalas, unlike the Shaivite Cholas, were a Vaishnavite house influenced by Sri Ramanuja (1077-1157), who stressed bhakti (devotion) as a means to salvation.

In the Deccan, too, this was a time of change; the Yadavas, or Seuna, based in Devagiri (now Daulatabad), expanded as far north as Gujarat.

During the entire medieval period, towns continued to increase in importance. For instance, the Jain pilgrimage center Shravanabelagola developed from a pure shrine into a major merchant town. The establishment of trading associations and local craft guilds show that commercial success now forced artisans and merchants to create new institutions to manage their businesses; however, they do not seem to have aspired to political power.

At the same time, there was a striking increase in temple building. Tanjore's temple received donations from as far away as Sri Lanka, while Rajendra Chola (Rajaraja's son) founded a massive temple at Gongaikondacholapuram, a mouthful that means "The City to which the Cholas brought the Ganges" since he had conquered Odisha and Bengal and had pots of Ganges water sent back to his capital. (Rajendra also conquered Srivijaya and part of Burma, a rare act of foreign expansionism; most Indian kings restricted their ambitions to the subcontinent.)

Rock-cut temples gave way to freestanding temple buildings by the end of the period, often with multiple concentric courtyards surrounding the temple (as at Srirangam, where the temple occupies 155 acres with seven concentric enclosures). The main temple spire often reached impressive heights, but it was now also surrounded by gopuras, or gateway towers, often at all four cardinal directions. Large halls were added for recitations of devotional poetry. Temple communities developed to a huge size; Tanjore's main temple had 600 employees, including dancers, cooks, and musicians, as well as priests.

A gopura at the Sri Ranganathasamy Temple Rajagopuram, Srirangam, Tiruchirapalli
Writer hit, CC BY-SA 4.0 <https://creativecommons.org/licenses/by-sa/4.0>, via Wikimedia Commons; https://commons.wikimedia.org/wiki/File:Srirangam_Temple_Gopuram_View.jpg

The Tamil poets, known as the Alvars (Vaishnavite) and Nayanars (Shaivite), flourished in the early Middle Ages, writing devotional poetry that influenced the bhakti movement. Their work often draws a parallel between kings and gods; the temple is shown as the palace of the deity, and the idol is given a lifestyle like a king's.

Northern India in the Middle Ages

Meanwhile, in northern India, three great empires overlapped: the Rashtrakuta in the Deccan, the Gurjara-Pratiharas in Malwa (today's Madhya Pradesh) and Gujarat, and the Pala or Dharma kings in Bengal and Bihar. Kannauj, the city where the three realms met, was the focal point of the conflict between them, which is often referred to as the Tripartite Struggle.

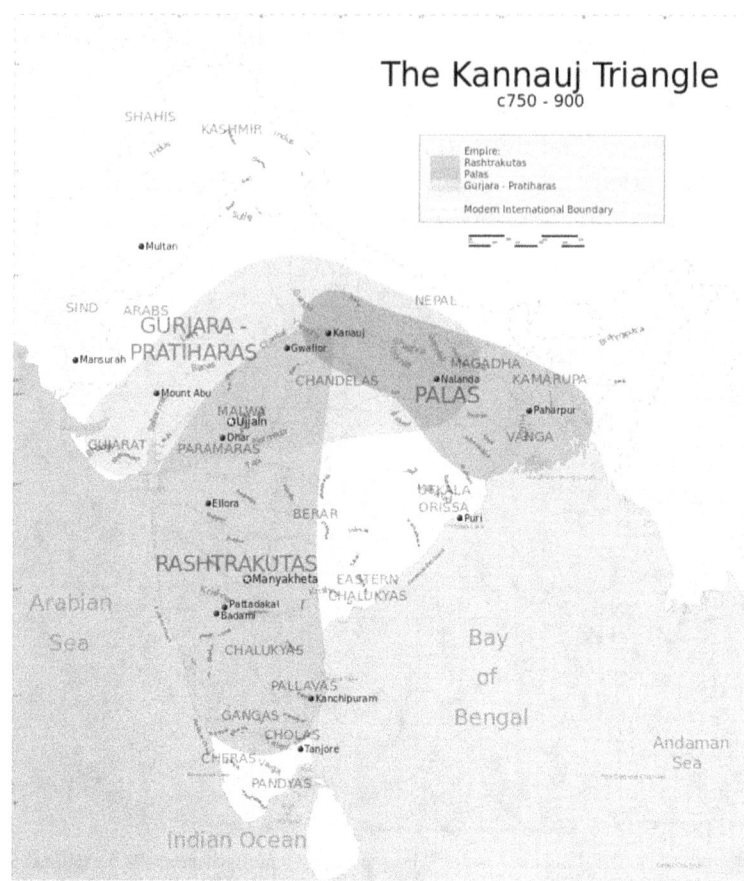

The Tripartite Struggle between three kingdoms. Note how Kannauj is right in the middle of the disputed area.
w:user:Planemad, CC BY-SA 3.0 <https://creativecommons.org/licenses/by-sa/3.0>, via Wikimedia Commons; https://commons.wikimedia.org/wiki/File:Indian_Kanauj_triangle_map.svg

The Pala dynasty greatly increased the agricultural exploitation of the eastern Indo-Gangetic Plain with widespread rice cultivation. They also had commercial interests in Southeast Asia, and their wealth enabled them to give significant patronage to Buddhist institutions such as the university at Nalanda. However, their attempts to push south were repelled by the Chola; this seems to have set quite a firm line between north and south.

In the northwest, Rajput clans became dominant, many of them claiming descent from the sun god Surya (as the Maharanas of Mewar, in Udaipur, still do) or from Rama. Others said they were descended from a sacrificial fire on Mount Abu. The rulers may not originally have been from the Kshatriya caste, but their newly-created genealogies, together with the acquiescence of the Brahmin priests, enabled them to step up to their new caste and legitimize their rule.

This northern society appears to have been less developed than in the south. For instance, hero stones marking the memory of heroes killed in battle or in cattle raids are found two centuries later in the Rajput territories than in southern India. Land ownership was also considerably less developed in terms of types of tenure.

Northern temple architecture developed in a different style than in the south. The basics of the temple are similar: there is a cave-like shrine with a shikhara spire over it, preceded by one or more vestibules, often with a walkway around the sanctuary. Unlike southern straight-sided towers, the shikhara is usually curved. The biggest difference from the southern style is that the whole temple is usually raised on a high plinth, giving it a much more impressive profile. Towards the end of the Middle Ages, highly ornate carving became usual. Perhaps the best example is the Dilwara Jain Temple complex on Mount Abu, which has minutely detailed, delicate carvings in fine white marble.

In Orissa, the temples of Bhubaneshwar, the Jagannath Temple in Puri, and the Sun Temple of Konarak all date from this period. In Bundelkhand, the Chandela dynasty built the Khajuraho temples, including both Jain and Hindu sanctuaries, which are notorious for their erotic imagery.

The Jagannath Temple in Puri by night. Note the pyramidal mandapa roofs and the curved sides of the shikhara spire.
Kalyanpuranand, CC BY-SA 4.0 <https://creativecommons.org/licenses/by-sa/4.0>, via Wikimedia Commons; https://commons.wikimedia.org/wiki/File:Lord_Jagannath_temple_at_night.jpg

However, while the balance of power teetered between these various Indian dynasties, a new threat was massing on the northern frontier. India was used to trading with the Arabs and saw them as a source of revenue, but the Turkic Muslims of Central Asia were a different kettle of fish—they were intent on raiding, not trading. Mahmud of Ghazni led seventeen separate raids down from the barren Hindu Kush into India; in 1018, he destroyed Mathura, taking away huge amounts of gold and silver. In 1023, it was Gwalior's turn, which decided to pay him protection money rather than risk seeing its city sacked. In 1025, Mahmud raided Gujarat and destroyed the Somnath Temple, taking its great doors. (Lord Ellenborough, believing that Mahmud had reused these doors in his mausoleum in Afghanistan, had them ripped off during the Battle of Kabul in 1842 and brought back to India. However, they are clearly northern since they're made of deodar wood, and deodars don't grow in Gujarat. They're also clearly ornamented in an Islamic style, with geometrical figures such as six-pointed stars. They are now kept in a side room at Agra Fort.)

Muhammad Ghuri, who invaded at the end of the twelfth century, took things a step further than simply raiding. Rather than going home with the loot, he intended from the first to create his own kingdom in India. In 1182, he conquered Sind and then started looking farther south. While at the First Battle of Tarain in 1191, he was unsuccessful; after the Second Battle of Tarain in 1192, he was able to take control of Delhi. Ghori was assassinated in 1206, so he didn't get to enjoy his new sultanate all that long, but the damage had been done. The Delhi Sultanate now became the nucleus of a new political entity and of the Muslim religion in India; it also became a staging post for further expeditions south as far as Karnataka, where five separate Bahmani sultanates emerged.

In the south, the Vijayanagar Empire had become prominent in the late Middle Ages, leaving the immense ruins of its capital Vijayanagara at Hampi. For a long time, Vijayanagar held out, sometimes playing one sultanate against another, but eventually, the five Bahmani sultanates banded together against the empire; they destroyed it in the Battle of Talikota in 1565. (Today, it's one of the chief backpacker centers in India, with its ruins spread out over several square miles along the Tungabhadra River.)

Culturally, the highlight of this era was the bhakti movement. Rather than stressing ritual, it stressed the direct relationship between the bhakta (devotee) and their god. Many bhakti devotional poems are written as love poems. Women and lower castes were liberated from the constraints of Brahmanical demands for "purity" and took an active role in the movement.

Sri Ramanuja (1077-1157) gave this tradition a philosophical underpinning. For him, salvation (moksha) couldn't be achieved simply through knowledge but must come through bhakti yoga, the discipline of devotion. He saw moksha not simply as freedom from further rebirths but as a state of joy in which the soul can continuously contemplate and enjoy divine perfection. He also fought for the lower castes to be admitted to temples and for non-Brahmins to be involved in the practice of puja.

Jayadeva's Gita Govinda, written in the twelfth century, is a set of poems telling the story of Radha's love for Krishna. Their separations and eventual reconciliation are symbolic of the soul's distraction from the love of god and its eventual return through devotion; in many ways, Radha becomes a symbol of and role model for the bhakta. Each poem has its raga or musical mode noted, and Jayadeva is said to have sung one of the compositions each night in the temple of Jagannath at Puri, a tradition that continues today.

Chaitanya Mahaprabhu (1486-1534) was born in Bengal and became an ecstatic devotee of Krishna; some people even regarded him as an avatar of Krishna. It is Chaitanya who was responsible for rediscovering the sacred forests around Vrindavan, where Krishna spent his life with Radha and the gopis (cow-girls); he also popularized the chanting of Hare Krishna.

Even Muslims could follow the path of bhakti. Kabir, born in 1398, was the son of a Muslim weaver, but his poetry dismisses both Muslim and Hindu rites and dogma and advocates looking into the devotee's own heart to find the presence of god. Both Hindus and Muslims disowned him while he was alive and claimed him after his death; the Sikhs later included some of his poetry in their scripture, the Adi Granth.

In some ways, Guru Nanak, the founder of Sikhism, can be seen as coming from a bhakti tradition. He was born in 1469 in Punjab to a merchant family and developed a spirituality based on the equality of all believers, good actions, and fraternity. He traveled extensively, visiting major pilgrimage centers of both Hindu and Muslim faiths, and emphasized bhakti as a way of integrating spiritual practice into practical daily life.

Originally, Sikhism was a peaceful religion, but persecution of the Sikhs from the time of emperor Jahangir turned the Sikhs into a militant sect. (This will be covered in the next chapter). The Guru Granth Sahib, the scripture of the Sikhs, is a pluralistic work; it's written in Gurmukhi script but includes Persian, Braj Bhasha, Prakrit, and Sanskrit texts, as well as Punjabi; it also includes verses by Kabir and the Hindu bhakti poet Ravidas, as well as teaching from the Islamic mystic, Baba Farid.

Chapter 4: The Mughal Empire: A Struggle for Supremacy

The Mughal Empire is perhaps one of the world's most well-known early modern empires, but its roots were in failure. The failure was Babur, prince of Fergana and great-great-great-grandson of Timur, or Tamerlane as he was known to the West.

Timur was a spectacularly successful man. He was a Turkic nomad who managed to conquer the Chagatai Khanate, which descended from Genghis Khan. He then led military campaigns across Central Asia, becoming the leading ruler of the Islamic world and making his capital in Samarkand. Timur actually invaded India and sacked Delhi in 1398. Understanding that elephants were easily panicked, he put his enemy's forces to rout by sending fire camels against them—that is, camels with hay piled high on their backs and then set on fire. However, other things soon distracted Timur from pursuing his Indian excursion.

Babur took after Timur in being valiant and smart but was, unfortunately, a serial failure. He won Samarkand but then he lost Fergana; he then managed to lose Samarkand three separate times. Clearly, Timur's inheritance was not going to fall into his hands. In the end, he decided to turn east and then south, taking Kabul, where he set up his rule, and then heading into India. And there, finally, his luck began to change.

Babur is a fascinating figure. He left an autobiography, the Baburnama, which is a strange mix of diplomacy, warfare, and natural history. On one page, he describes how his men built a tower of severed enemy heads after a battle; on the next, he discusses where to find the best muskmelons or describes different varieties of parrots. In between, he did a lot of partying: the founder of the Mughal Empire was, in fact, a drug fiend.

It took him five separate expeditions to figure out that India was not just a source of wealth and bananas but a good place to create a new empire. The Delhi sultanate had always been weakened by dissension and dynastic squabbles, making it a clear target, so that was where he focused. In the Battle of Panipat of 1526, Babur defeated Ibrahim Lodi of Delhi, and the Delhi sultanate became the beginning of the Mughal Empire.

However, Delhi was a small place, and it was surrounded by enemies, including the Rajputs in the north, who could easily cut it off from Kabul. The Rajputs were a much stronger enemy than the Delhi sultanate. Rana Sanga of Mewar (Udaipur) succeeded in getting the different Rajput clans to unite against the invader, creating a 200,000-strong army. (Numbers at this period are always approximate and often exaggerated, and it's Babur who gives this number, so take it with a grain of salt.)

At the Battle of Khanwa (1527), Babur, a fine strategist, built a fortified position and raked the Rajputs with artillery and musket fire without engaging in close combat. This allowed him to draw the sting of the Rajput charge. He also kept his horsemen back, ready for a flanking move. Only when the Rajputs attacked the Mughal flanks did Babur loose his army on them; Rana Sanga was shot and concussed, and Babur took advantage of the resulting confusion to take the offensive and completely rout the Rajput forces.

Panipat is often considered one of the most important battles ever fought in India. Arguably, though, Khanwa was even more important. It brought Hindu rulers under Babur's empire, and Babur, being a smart ruler, accepted Hindus into both his army and his administration. The Mughal Empire became a mixed empire where all faiths were tolerated and a major trading center, exporting prettily painted and embroidered cloth to Europe. (The French called these "indiennes," while the English called them by their Hindi name, "chintz.")

Babur's version of Islam was liberal. He used drugs and drank alcohol, and like the Persians of his day, he saw nothing wrong in figurative art or music. The Taliban would definitely not have approved. He did, however, impose the jizya tax on non-Muslims in his empire.

Babur died in 1530 at just 47, having turned his initial failure into brilliant success. His son Humayun, unfortunately, was not able to keep things together. First, he was challenged for the throne by his brothers Kamran, Askari, and Hindal. Then he was pushed out of India again by Sher Shah Suri, a warlord who had created his own state in Bengal. He spent many years in Persia, where Shah Tahmasp gave him refuge.

But in 1555, Humayun was able to reclaim his throne, as well as his son Akbar, who had been left behind in Kabul when Humayun fled. He lasted less than a year, slipping on the steps of his library and dying of his injuries three days later.

Akbar succeeded to the throne at just thirteen years old. He was an unruly, self-willed, obstinate, and functionally illiterate boy, but he also had vast physical courage and daring and intense curiosity. He rode male elephants in musth (an aggressive, testosterone-fueled mood), swam rivers swollen with monsoon rains, and occasionally went berserk with rage. But he was also intelligent and learned quickly. By relying on speed and firepower and introducing innovations such as camel and elephant-mounted swiveling guns, he changed the rules of war and made his forces virtually impossible to defeat. He even invented rockets with shrieking whistles tied to them, which would drive his enemies' horses mad with their wailing sound.

Akbar with a lion and a lamb, from an album belonging to Shah Jahan. It clearly shows the eclectic nature of the Mughal court, with little angels in the sky and a crown clearly copied from European originals.

CC0 1.0 Universal (CC0 1.0) Public Domain Dedication https://creativecommons.org/publicdomain/zero/1.0/ https://www.lookandlearn.com/history-images/YM0451268/Akbar-With-Lion-and-Calf-Folio-from-the-Shah-Jahan-Album)

Akbar wasn't just a military genius; he was also a smart ruler like his grandfather. For instance, he realized that as long as the empire relied only on central Asian nobles (the Turani), it would not be easy to govern and would not have support from the people. To end the Turanis' dominance, he brought in Persian and Rajput administrators and created the mansab system in which land grants (jagirs) were related to the rank of the holder and were regularly rotated rather than hereditary. He also started minting square rupees, creating a coinage that could soon be used across his entire empire and abolishing the jizya tax on Hindus.

Though initially ruling only in name, Akbar soon took over for his regent and expanded his empire. In 1567, he took the fortress of Chittor, formerly considered impregnable; he had already taken Mandu, Malwa, and Gondwana. After this, several other Rajput rajas decided to join the Mughals voluntarily, bringing Bikaner, Bundelkhand, and Jaisalmer under his control. At Chittor, the women of the fort committed jauhar, immolating themselves in a fire while the men dressed in holy saffron garments and issued out of the fort on what was clearly a suicide mission. (This may well have shocked Akbar as much as it shocks us; he passed a law against women being forced to commit sati, though allowing voluntary sati.)

Akbar also married a Rajput woman, Harkha Bai, known in the Mughal court as Mariam-uz-Zamani, who was the mother of the next emperor, Jahangir. Other Rajput wives followed, bringing their own religion and customs to the Mughal court. Thus, instead of being an Islamic conqueror, Akbar became the head of a mixed-race, mixed-religion, syncretic court.

At his new capital of Fatehpur Sikri, Akbar created a new kind of architecture, again mixing influences from Islamic Central Asia with native Indian styles. His buildings have Indian chhatri pavilions but also huge arches, which come from Iranian mosque styles. In the Diwan-i-Khas, his private audience hall, four stone walkways in the air connected stairs at the corners of the building to a central column supporting Akbar's throne, a stunning and unique conception of the emperor seated in the air. (The palace also included a small temple where his Hindu wife could worship.) There are also domes, which were unknown in India before the Mughals but became a regular motif of Mughal architecture.

Akbar may also have invented his own religion, though this depends on how you interpret his desire for sulh-i-kul, "universal harmony." Some historians have suggested that he set up a syncretist religion in which he served as a deputy for god. It's perhaps more likely that he had a small clique with special admissions rituals within which he and members of his court conducted their spiritual investigations—a religious club, so to speak, rather than a cult. What's certain is that in addition to taking Hindus into his court, Akbar welcomed at least three Jesuit missionaries, as well as Jewish scholars, to his debates. His curiosity was intense, and this included religion, as well as warfare and architecture.

This was a golden age of the arts. The environment in Persia was becoming increasingly intolerant, which allowed Akbar to recruit many Persian artists and artisans; he also brought the famed musician Tansen from Gwalior and hired Indian painters. Though he was illiterate, Akbar loved to be read to, and he sponsored the translation of works like the Mahabharata from the Indian languages into Persian.

Akbar was not the first Mughal emperor, but he was the first wholly Indian Mughal emperor. Under him, India became the center of the world economically, greater than any other empire of the time. And it continued to increase in size. In 1575, he took Bihar and Bengal from the Afghan chief Daud Khan, and the next year he defeated his last major Rajput opponent, Rana Pratap of Mewar, in the Battle of Haldighati. (Cannily, he sent the Rajput general Kunwar Man Singh to lead the Mughal army, encouraging his Hindu officers to fight well against another Rajput.) Then, in 1585, he took Kashmir and, in the 1590s, looked to the Deccan, where the Bahmani sultanate had fragmented.

Salim, one of Akbar's three sons, set up his own court at Allahabad in 1600 in what was an understated form of rebellion. But Akbar, perhaps influenced by the women of his harem, remained diplomatic and didn't push Salim into open opposition. When Akbar died in 1605, Salim inherited his empire, taking the name Jahangir, "Conqueror of the World."

Jahangir continued his father's artistic patronage and policy of mixing different religions and cultures. He also accepted the first English ambassador, Sir Thomas Roe, in 1615 and gave him permission for an English "factory" (trading house) at Surat. In his diary, Roe claims that he and the emperor were drinking buddies. However, Jahangir doesn't mention Roe at all in his autobiography.

Like his father Akbar, Jahangir had married a number of Rajput princesses. This tied the Rajput princely houses even more tightly into the

Mughal empire. He later married the widow of a Persian officer, Sher Afgan; her name was Nur Jahan, and as Jahangir's twentieth and last wife, she became the power behind the throne, placing members of her family in high offices. She was, apparently, an excellent tiger hunter and keen shot.

Nur Jahan and her father, Mirza Ghiyas Beg (also known by his honorific title of I'timad-ud-Daulah, "Pillar of the State"), became the power behind the throne. Jahangir had inherited Babur's and Akbar's predilections for drugs and alcohol but not their strength of will, so letting Nur Jahan take over much of the business of state was tempting. It also wasn't the worst thing he could have done; Nur Jahan had been well educated by her father and was highly capable as an administrator. She even rescued her husband from captivity when rebels attacked his caravan on the way to Kashmir.

Jahangir died in 1627 without having chosen a successor. Nur Jahan supported prince Shahryar, who had married her daughter Ladli. However, Prince Khurram defeated and executed Shahryar and succeeded to the throne as Shah Jahan ("King of the World"). Nur Jahan spent the rest of her life under house arrest in Lahore.

Shah Jahan is now best remembered as the emperor who built the Taj Mahal for his favorite wife, Mumtaz Mahal. The story of their marriage is one of India's great love stories, but to avoid being too sentimental, it's worth remembering that they had fourteen children, and Mumtaz Mahal died giving birth to the fourteenth. Her body must have been exhausted.

The Taj Mahal, epitome of Mughal architecture and gardening.
This file is not in the public domain. Therefore you are requested to use the following next to the image if you reuse this file: © Yann Forget / Wikimedia Commons.
https://commons.wikimedia.org/wiki/File:Taj_Mahal_(Edited).jpeg

The Taj Mahal marks the summit of Mughal architecture. While Akbar's architecture was a blend of Indian and Central Asian elements, by Shah Jahan's rule, the two currents had fused into one, and the mausoleum is a completely integrated architectural concept. It uses a rhythmic combination of solids and voids and concave and convex elements, such as the nine open arches in the façade. While on Akbar's mausoleum the little chhatri pavilions all stand separately, the Taj Mahal integrates the four corner domes so they form a pyramidal massing with the main dome.

The pietra dura work of inlaid marble and semiprecious stones is particularly notable, showing naturalistic flowers and making the entire work a reference to the gardens of paradise. All the Mughal emperors from Babur onward loved gardens. The square garden with a building at its center and watercourses for cooling was one of the most delightful contributions of Mughal culture.

After the syncretic and tolerant reigns of the previous two emperors, under Shah Jahan, the Mughal Empire turned back towards Islamic orthodoxy. He also expanded the empire in the south, subduing three of the Deccan sultanates, and defeated a Sikh rebellion in Punjab under Guru Hargobind.

But in 1658, Shah Jahan became seriously ill. He would, in fact, live another seven years, but his illness set off a fratricidal struggle between the crown prince and regent Dara Shukoh and his younger brothers Shuja, Murad Bakhsh, and Aurangzeb. After defeating Dara Shukoh at the Battle of Samugarh, Aurangzeb became the sixth Mughal emperor, declaring his father incompetent to rule and shutting him up in Agra Fort for the rest of his life. (From the fort, Shah Jahan would have seen the Taj Mahal every day, just the other side of the river Yamuna.)

Under Aurangzeb, the Mughal Empire reached its full extent, taking Ladakh (in the Himalayas) as a tributary state and conquering Bengal and the remaining southern sultanates of Bijapur and Golconda (Hyderabad).

However, Aurangzeb finally broke with the Mughal tradition of tolerance. He brought back the jizya, the extra tax on non-Muslims, as well as a super-tax on the profits of Hindu merchants. (He was probably short of funds after the intense warfare preceding his coming to power. However, one result of his policies, and of an increase in land tax, was that many Hindus decided to emigrate to lands under the jurisdiction of the East India Company, where there were no religion-based taxes.)

Aurangzeb also demolished a number of Hindu temples; he was apparently concerned about Muslims who were attracted by Hindu teachings and adopted non-Muslim ways of life or dress. He also executed "heretic" Muslims, such as the Sufi mystic Sarmad Kashani, executed Dara Shukoh on the grounds of apostasy, and had the Sikh Guru Tegh Bahadur put to death.

In particular, Aurengzeb demolished the temple of Vishwanath at Varanasi, and the temple at Mathura, which contained the site of Krishna's birthplace. Some earlier temple destructions can be attributed to the desire of a conqueror to destroy the works of previous rulers. Even some Hindu rulers did this: for instance, Indra III Rashtrakuta destroyed the Pratihara-founded temple at Kalpa. But in the case of Aurangzeb, contemporary documentation shows that his destruction of these temples was motivated purely by religious doctrine. His demolitions of these two important centers of Hindu worship are still a sore point with Hindus today.

But Aurengzeb died a disappointed man. Shivaji and his Marathas were pressing on one side, a Pashtun rebellion in Afghanistan on the other. His interminable wars had impoverished his empire. When he died at the age of 88, he had outlived many of his children and had not appointed a successor.

"I came alone and I go as a stranger," he wrote. "The instant which has passed in power has left only sorrow behind it. I have not been the guardian and protector of the Empire. Life, so valuable, has been squandered in vain. God was in my heart but I could not see him. Life is transient. The past is gone and there is no hope for the future. The whole imperial army is like me: bewildered, perturbed, separated from God, quaking like quicksilver. I fear my punishment. Though I have a firm hope in God's grace, yet for my deeds anxiety ever remains with me" (Dalrymple 2019). His grave, in the little town of Khuldabad, is a simple open-air tomb in the courtyard of a saint's shrine, far from the glories of his predecessors' tombs in Lahore, Delhi, and Agra.

After Aurangzeb's death in 1707, the Mughal state began to crumble. Aurangzeb had damaged the Mughal economy by pursuing an expensive military program; his expansion of the empire came at the expense of its solvency. He had also badly misjudged his sons, expecting them to share the empire among them. (Sharing never seemed to have been a Mughal trait. Aurangzeb should have remembered how he had killed his brothers to ascend to the throne.)

Akbar had ruled 49 years, Jahangir 21, Shah Jahan 30, and Aurangzeb 48. The next emperor, Aurangzeb's third son Azam Shah, ruled for only three months. Bahadur Shah, Aurangzeb's second son, beat Azam Shah in battle and took the throne but died four years later. Bahadur's son Jahandar Shah managed only 350 days before his nephew Farrukhsiyar defeated him in battle, imprisoned him, and then had him strangled.

It was Farrukhsiyar who gave the East India Company a license to trade tax-free in Bengal, Bihar, and Orissa, sowing the seeds of the Mughal Empire's doom. Already, uprisings of Jats, Sikhs, and the Marathas had challenged the empire, and various successor states now began to break away, too; the empire broke down into warring kingdoms. In 1739, the Persians under Nader Shah sacked the capital, Delhi, taking plunder that included Jahangir's Peacock Throne and the Koh-i-Noor diamond.

Between them, Jahangir and Aurangzeb had also managed to turn the Sikhs from peaceful coreligionists into a vengeful army by persecuting the new and relatively small sect. In 1606, Jahangir gave the fifth Sikh guru, Guru Arjan Dev, the choice of converting to Islam or being executed; the guru chose death. After this, Guru Arjan Dev's son and successor as the sixth guru, Guru Hargobind, created a Sikh army. He managed to maintain distant relations with Jahangir, but under Shah Jahan, the Sikhs waged open war against the Mughal Empire and local governors in Punjab. In 1675, Aurangzeb had the ninth Sikh guru, Guru Tegh Bahadur, executed (giving him the same choice Jahangir had given Guru Arjan Dec). After this event, the Sikh identity had been firmly forged not just as a religious but also as a political and military identity.

The Sikhs now depended on their military leaders rather than the gurus. Banda Singh Bahadur headed up the Khalsa (a Sikh community and army) in the early eighteenth century. He abolished the Mughal zamindari tax and land-holding system within Sikh lands, giving peasant farmers ownership of their own land, but he was eventually captured by the Mughals and executed.

After Banda Singh's time, the Sikhs retreated to the jungles and used guerrilla tactics against the Mughals; they were considered little better than bandits by the Mughal Empire. In 1716, Farrukhsiyar commanded that Sikhs, if found, would be either forcibly converted to Islam or executed.

However, by 1783, the battle-hardened Sikhs had turned the tables. Jassa Singh Ramgarhia led a Sikh army into Delhi, and the Mughals under

Shah Alam II were forced to make peace. The Sikh Confederacy was now in full control of Punjab. Ranjit Singh, leader of the largest part of the Sikh Confederacy, rose to power as leader of the entire community and, in 1801, was crowned as Maharaja of Punjab, creating the Sikh Empire, which he ruled until his death in 1839.

Maharaja Ranjit Singh, "Lion of the Punjab," from a contemporary portrait.
https://commons.wikimedia.org/wiki/File:Maharaj_Ranjit_Singh.jpg

(After Ranjit Singh's death, however, things fell apart remarkably quickly. There were poisoning, "accidents," assassinations, and four leaders in just two years. Duleep Singh, the last Maharaja, succeeded at the age of five in 1843. He was deposed by the British, then exiled to Britain, where he befriended Queen Victoria, hunted with the Prince of Wales, and was renowned as the fourth best shot in England. His son and successor, Victor Albert Jay Duleep Singh, went to Eton and Sandhurst and married into the British aristocracy; his daughter, Sophia Duleep Singh, became a prominent suffragette, and Catherine Duleep Singh moved to Germany, where she and her former governess helped save a number of Jewish families in the 1930s by helping them move to the UK.)

The late Mughal empire didn't just have the Sikhs to deal with in the north; it was being put under pressure from the south by the late seventeenth century, as well. Shivaji Bhonsle, son of an army officer who had worked for many different local rulers, decided to take advantage of the sultanate of Bijapur's weakness by taking a number of forts for himself. Eventually, Shivaji defeated Bijapur's forces at the Battle of Pratapgarh in 1659 and was then able to take much of the Konkan coast to the west.

Shivaji, with his Maratha followers, invaded the Deccan and headed for Surat in Gujarat. He attacked the Portuguese settlement in Basrur by sea but then had a setback: Aurangzeb's general Jai Singh forced him to a stalemate, and Shivaji signed the Treaty of Purandar, becoming a vassal of the Mughal Empire.

However, Aurangzeb made a bad mistake when he summoned Shivaji to court in 1666: he offended Shivaji by making him stand next to low-ranking men he had defeated in battle. Shivaji protested, refused to come to court again, and was then put under house arrest while Aurangzeb decided what to do with him.

Shivaji, a patient man and a good Hindu, made a practice of sending large baskets of sweets to priests and the poor while he was in prison. After a couple of months of piety, he knew that his jailers were used to seeing the baskets sent out and were no longer paying much attention. He hid in one, his son Sambhaji hid in another, and they were carried stickily to freedom.

Years of uneasy peace with the Mughals followed. Aurengzeb was fighting hard in the north and pulled troops out of the Deccan; many disbanded soldiers decided they would rather join the Marathas. Shivaji had soon retaken the Deccan and most of the coast from Surat nearly all the way down to Goa; eventually, he controlled the peninsula all the way across to Madras. He harassed the English factory in Bombay and invaded Bengal. Finally, he decided that he should be a king. Only one thing stood in his way: the fact that he was Shudra, not Kshatriya, by caste. The Brahmins of his court objected.

Shivaji found a friendly scholar from Varanasi who discovered a genealogy proving he was of royal blood. He was still made to do penance for not observing the correct caste rituals, go through the sacred thread ceremony, and then remarry all his wives according to the Vedic rites. Finally, in 1674, he was crowned king, and the Maratha Empire came into being. Tanjore (Thanjavur), too, came into the empire, then Mysore; the dream of a united south India was very nearly complete.

Shivaji died in 1680 and was succeeded by his sons Sambhaji and Rajaram, then his grandson Shahu. The Marathas very nearly took Delhi itself in 1737, by which time the Mughal Empire had been pushed right back to a small area around Delhi and Panipat, and most of the Muslim states had been conquered. Only the Nizam of Hyderabad had been able to hold out in the south—and would do so until India became independent and beyond.

The Maratha Empire eventually became a confederacy between the Gaekwads of Baroda, the Holkars of Indore and Malwa, the Bhonsales of Nagpur, and the Scindias of Gwalior. For a while, this delicate balancing act seemed to work. Then, suddenly, the British were there, pitting each of these princely families against the others—and the Maratha Empire vanished as quickly as it had come to be. But that's a story that opens a new chapter in India's history.

Chapter 5: Colonial India and the East India Company

The story of the British in India begins with the foundation of the East India Company (EIC or the Company) in 1600. At this time, England was wealthy under Queen Elizabeth I, Shakespeare was writing his plays, and England seemed to be on a roll—except that it had missed out on the wave of wealth coming to Spain and Portugal through the colonization of Latin America. London traders and their seafaring friends wanted something better, and to find it, they looked east, not west.

At first, they concentrated on setting up trading stations, known as "factories," enabling them to export Indian goods such as palampores (highly decorated cloth), cotton, silk, and indigo. (The Dutch had already taken control of the spice trade, concentrating on Indonesia.) In the early seventeenth century, trade was set up at Machilipatnam/Masulipatnam on the east coast, Surat in Gujarat, Burhampore and Cossimbazar in Bengal, Calicut/Kozhikode in Kerala, Patna, Madras/Chennai, and Dacca/Dhaka (now the capital of Bangladesh); in the later seventeenth century, Hooghly, Bombay/Mumbai, and Calcutta followed.

The EIC started small but grew rapidly. By 1750, the EIC made up nearly £1 million of Britain's total £8 million import trade, tea alone accounting for £0.5 million of revenue. Many Members of Parliament (MPs) and members of the House of Lords were shareholders in the EIC, so it had become, as it were, the tail that wagged the dog. If it needed legislation passed to support its aims, it had many "tame" MPs who would support it.

Even so, the EIC was simply a business investment company, an import/export business, so to speak. However, two major trends would eventually change the status of British involvement in India. The first was the gradual breakdown of the Mughal Empire. The second was the increasing tension between France and Britain, which became a global conflict fought out through the American War of Independence and in India.

The Carnatic Wars from 1746 to 1763 were sparked off by the War of the Austrian Succession in Europe. (This set France, Prussia, and Spain against the Habsburg monarchy and Britain, eventually involving most of Europe.)

Joseph François Dupleix, governor of the French East India Company, was an ambitious man and saw how he could expand French influence in India by attacking the British. While at first successful, he came up against the young Robert Clive.

Clive appears to have been something of a thug as a youngster. He was a troublemaker at school, always fighting, and his father may have sent him out to India because he simply didn't know what to do with him. He became a remarkably brave (even foolhardy) Company officer, though he had no military training—his first two years were spent mainly keeping the Company's accounts in Fort St. George (Madras). He was involved in the First Carnatic War when, in 1746, Madras was seized and the Company's officers taken to Pondicherry as captives. He managed to escape with three others dressed as Indians; later, he was given a platoon at the Siege of Pondicherry, where he distinguished himself in action.

In 1748, the death of the Nizam of Hyderabad set off the Second Carnatic War. Here, Clive really made his name, making several forced marches to take the fort of Arcot by surprise. When he was surrounded by besiegers, he waited for night and launched a surprise attack on the other army; they fled, never finding out how small his forces were. Surprise had become one of Clive's signature tactics. Eventually, French India was reduced to the single outpost of Pondicherry (where the bakers still serve excellent croissants and the policemen wear French-style képis).

Despite now being called "Clive of India" by the British public, Clive actually loathed India and was glad of the chance to retire to England, having made his fortune. He spent the next couple of years playing British politics—and losing. However, he was called back to India, and since he appears to have already spent a significant part of his fortune, he may have needed to take up his post again to receive fresh funds. He landed in Madras but, following the news that Cossimbazar and Calcutta had been taken by the Nawab of Bengal, was quickly sent north to deal with the situation.

Mughal Bengal was ruled from Murshidabad and had allowed numerous factories to be set up along the Hooghly River by the Portuguese, Dutch, and Armenians, as well as the English. This was, at the time, one of the richest areas of India, with a huge textile trade, and the Nawabs had created a courtly culture of some sophistication. The provinces of Bihar, Bengal, and Orissa (from 1741) were ruled by Nawab Alivardi Khan, who maintained strict neutrality with the European nations that traded in Bengal; unlike the south, Bengal had escaped involvement in the wars between France and Britain. (Alivardi was a cat-lover and often did business with a white Persian cat on his lap—a Mughal version of the James Bond series' Ernest Blofeld!)

For finance, Alivardi also relied on the Seth family of bankers. They acted as the central treasury, and controlled the mint selling currency to the EIC and making a commission on this supply. The Seth bank had branches in several Company towns, such as Calcutta, Surat, Bombay, and Madras.

However, Alivardi died in 1756, and his successor, his 23-year-old nephew Siraj ud-Daulah, did not follow Alivardi's cautious policies. He has often been dismissed as a drunkard and even presented as a serial bisexual rapist and psychopath (Dalrymple, 2019). Siraj had made himself persona non grata with the British through his intemperate behavior and, determined to teach them a lesson, marched on first on Cossimbazar and then Calcutta.

The British were overwhelmed; Fort William was not well-equipped, and the governor, Roger Drake, decided to flee with a number of officers. A surgeon, John Holwell, took command of the men who were left and formally surrendered to Siraj ud-Daulah. At first, the men were well treated, but after a few soldiers got drunk and started making themselves obnoxious, the British were rounded up and put into the prison of their own fort, the famous "Black Hole of Calcutta." The night was one of the hottest of the year, and after a night packed into the small room without water or fresh air, many of the men suffocated.

The Black Hole was not particularly celebrated at the time, but in Victorian India, it became a classic symbol of Indian barbarity and backwardness. However, it is worth remembering that the Black Hole was created by the British, and they thought it perfectly adequate for holding prisoners—although perhaps not in such high numbers. In recent years, the numbers cited by Holwell have also been challenged. According to him, only 23 of 146 people forced into the cell survived the night, but other historians have assessed the number of prisoners at the much lower 64 and 43.

One Bengali historian decided to take an experimental approach, marking off a square the same size as the cell, 18 square feet. He then asked local villagers to fill the space. Even though the Bengali villagers were probably smaller and thinner than the British soldiers had been and pushed as tightly together as possible, he could not manage to get 146 of them into the space.

Had Siraj ud-Daulah only upset the British, he might have survived. But he also upset the Jagat Seth ("Banker of the World") Mahtab Rai, his treasurer. When he couldn't get enough money out of the treasury, he slapped the Seth in public, making a formidable enemy of his main financier. He also replaced his paymaster, Mir Jafar. That was unwise; the Seths then decided they would work secretly for the British, and Mir Jafar joined the conspiracy. (He also had his eyes on the Nawab's throne.)

Clive quickly managed to retake Calcutta. Then, he took the French enclave of Chandannagar and declared war on Siraj ud-Daulah, marching his army up the Hooghly River toward Murshidabad. At Plassey, he found the Nawab's army already entrenched, with reinforcements expected to arrive in two days. Clive had his army take up position in a mango grove near a hunting lodge. His army was hugely outnumbered and tired, having crossed the river in spate to get to Plassey.

Siraj ud-Daulah's army was big, but Clive had a secret advantage. Mir Jafar, who led a large part of Siraj ud-Daulah's army, had pledged that his troops would not engage in the fight, but he would keep them standing by. He had also bribed other officers in the Bengali army. Everything hinged on whether Clive's allies in the Bengali camp would keep their word.

At daybreak on June 23, 1757, Siraj's artillery opened fire. The barrage continued all morning, but Siraj did not charge. After half an hour, Clive moved his men into the mango grove, which was protected by an embankment from the worst of the shelling. Mir Jafar was there with his division of the army but had not actively engaged in the battle. (Was he just biding his time or actively helping the English?)

At noon, it started to rain. Siraj had taken no precautions against the rain, and his artillery found its ammunition had gotten wet and would not fire. Meanwhile, Clive, who had not started to fire until now, and whose artillery was well-protected by tarpaulins, was able to commence continuous fire on the Nawab's army.

At this point, Mir Madan, the Bengali artillery chief, decided to attack the British, leading the charge on his war elephant. Thanks to a sharpshooting Company soldier, Mir Madan was shot and carried to the Nawab's tent, where he died. This turned the course of the battle; Siraj ud-Daulah seems to have lost all confidence and decided to retreat. Finally, Mir Jafar's men marched away, leaving Clive the victor.

Plassey cost the Nawab 500 men, including some of his best officers, such as Mir Madan, and three elephants. Only 22 British soldiers died, though 50 were wounded. Plassey opened the way to Murshidabad, where Mir Jafar had Siraj ud-Daulah murdered and then took power.

If Siraj had won the battle of Plassey, the EIC in Bengal would have been wiped out (and so would Mir Jafar, most likely). It was a desperate throw of the dice by Clive, but it worked. The Company was no longer just a trading house but a regional power in India. It was Clive, and not the Mughal emperor, who authorized Mir Jafar's coronation as Nawab. As a result, it was a multinational corporation and not the Mughal Empire that held political power. Bengal had effectively submitted to a corporate takeover.

In the future, the Company would continue to work through "tame" local rulers. For instance, in 1765, Sir Hector Munro defeated Shuja ud-Daulah, the Nawab of Awadh (Oudh), at Buxar; Clive reinstalled him as a "tame" Nawab, and Awadh remained a close ally of the Company for over a century. (Incidentally, Clive enriched himself by what we'd now call insider trading. When he heard of the victory at Buxar, he ordered his agent in England to mortgage his house and invest the funds in Company shares. He must have made a fortune on the deal.) The capture of Awadh gave the British huge leverage over the Mughals. The emperor, Shah Alam II, was prevailed upon to give the British the diwani rights to Bengal, Bihar, and Orissa, effectively making them governors of the province and giving them the right to collect tax revenue.

Clive returned to Britain as one of the richest men in the country, but he was not a happy man, and in 1774, he cut his throat with a penknife. He was only 49.

Bengal saw miserable times following the battle of Plassey. Clive's gamble had been costly, and the Company needed to gain a return on its investment. The easiest way of doing so was not through trade but by taxation. Bengal was bled white.

Unfortunately, by 1769, climatic conditions were changing. There was no rainfall; without rain, rice became short. By the end of 1770, famine had killed as many as ten million, a third of the population. Unlike Indian rulers, the British had not set up strategic rice reserves or charitable distribution networks. The Company's huge debts still had to be serviced, while the famine meant no tax revenues were coming in. Having killed millions of Indians, the Company managed to nearly kill itself: by 1773, it had to be bailed out by the British government.

Clive had identified several gifted men within the Company. One of these was Warren Hastings, whom Clive had made the British resident at Murshidabad. Hastings was very different from Clive; he was a scholar and a diligent manager, and he fell in love with India, quickly learning Persian, Urdu, and later Bengali. He also made a number of reforms. Clive had already created a modern army for the EIC, but Hastings transformed its bureaucracy and improved British knowledge about the subcontinent. He codified the laws, started the cartographical survey of India, and created a postal service. He also founded the Asiatic Society and sponsored a translation of the Bhagavad Gita. And he built huge granaries, including the immense Golghar in Patna (which can still be seen today), to avoid any future famine becoming as bad as the one in 1769-70.

Warren Hastings, painted by Tilly Kettle. This pensive and unassuming man ran India, and his second wife was a German baroness.
https://commons.wikimedia.org/wiki/File:Warren_Hastings_by_Tilly_Kettle.jpg

In 1773, Madras, Bombay, and Calcutta were brought under unified control with Hastings' appointment as governor-general; the Company became a single power rather than a trio of separate enclaves. Having been bailed out by the British government, it had also, in some sense, been nationalized. Though it retained autonomy, the government could now pull the strings.

Bengal and northern India were pretty much under British control, or at least influence, by now; this made the next major area for British expansion the south, where Haidar Ali and his son Tipu Sultan of Mysore formed a determined opposition to the Company. Haidar Ali had adopted modern military techniques from the French army in India, so his kingdom was not an easy conquest. In fact, there appears to have been a Jacobin club of French Republican officers in Mysore; Tipu is said to have planted a tree of liberty and declared himself "Citizen Tipu"—though this latter event may have been Company propaganda.

For a long time, the Mysore Sultans successful stopped the British, but in 1792, General Lord Cornwallis finally managed to take Bangalore. Even so, he could not take Tipu's fortress at Srirangapatna. Tipu still had to surrender, ceding half his territory.

Things were left to rest for a while, but once again, European events dictated the course of events in India: Nelson's victory at the Battle of Trafalgar in 1798 deprived Tipu of potential further French support, and Marquess Wellesley, with his brother Arthur (later the Duke of Wellington) on his staff, decided to go on the offensive now that Tipu was isolated. They took Srirangapatna on May 4, 1799, after a siege of nearly a month. Tipu, a fighter to the last, was killed defending the walls of his fort.

One small but intriguing souvenir of Tipu's court can now be found in the Victoria and Albert Museum in London—Tipu's tiger. The tiger was the emblem of Tipu's dynasty. His men wore tiger-striped tunics, there were tiger stripes on his coins, and his throne had tiger-headed arms. This beautifully carved and painted wooden tiger is shown in the act of killing an East India Company soldier, whose dying moans are imitated by the pipe organ hidden inside the tiger.

The Scindias and the Holkars were now the last remnants of the Maratha Empire, the Holkars ruling from Indore and the Scindias in Ujjain and later in Gwalior. Yashwantrao Holkar tried but failed to unite the remaining Maratha rulers and was ultimately prevailed upon to sign the Treaty of Rajghat in 1805, recognizing him as sovereign king but allying him with the British.

The Third Anglo-Maratha War in 1818 saw the conquest of the remaining Marathas, after which Indore and Gwalior became princely states under British rule. Bundelkhand, most of Rajasthan, and Nagpur all became British territories at the same time. Over the years, British India expanded its scope through alliances with states such as Cochin, Travancore (now Kerala), and Hyderabad. The East India Company had started as several tiny, isolated islands within India; now, it controlled – whether by conquest or alliance–virtually the whole subcontinent.

At the same time, the nature of British involvement in India was changing. Previously, many British Company employees had settled in India, marrying Indian women and often living the life of an Indian noble. Cornwallis put an end to that: he decreed that the British were not to settle in India. They became an expatriate community, returning to Britain after their tours of duty. This automatically downgraded the status of Anglo-Indian families. It also led to a wider social barrier between the British and the Indians; British clubs and social networks excluded Indians. The governor-general and later viceroy, for instance, was always a temporary appointment, normally a five-year term; the longest-serving was Lord Linlithgow, with just eight years of total service. Many Viceroys had not visited India before their appointment and consequently often had a poor understanding of the country they ruled.

Cornwallis also carried out land reforms that started to change the social makeup of India. His land reforms ruined many old Mughal families, and the Hindu bhadraloks (equivalent to "gentlemen") emerged to fill their place.

Cornwallis' intention with his various changes was probably to avoid India becoming like America, where English settlers had become more attached to America than their country of origin. However, his reforms led to India being administered by men who had no long-term interest in, or love for, the country.

The Company remained in control until 1857, although it was increasingly influenced by the British government's priorities. However, 1857 was a traumatic year and marked a decisive change in the nature of British rule. This was the year of what earlier British historians call the Sepoy Rebellion (Indian soldiers in the Company army were known as sepoys) but is now more frequently referred to as the Indian Rebellion of 1857; it can also be seen as the first war of independence.

There were many reasons for the rebellion. High taxes, reforms such as banning sati (widows joining their husbands on the funeral pyre), and rumors of forced conversions to Christianity had all alienated Indians. The Doctrine of Lapse, which allowed the British to take over princely states without a direct heir, was another sore point. And the Bengal army, recruited mainly from the higher castes, had grievances, such as being expected to serve overseas without the traditional special overseas payment.

The immediate spark for the rebellion was the introduction of the new Enfield rifle. This rifle used ready-prepared cartridges wrapped in greased paper; the end of the cartridge had to be bitten off before inserting it into the gun. The soldiers of the Bengal Army based at Meerut, near Delhi, heard that the cartridges were greased with beef tallow (forbidden to Hindus) and pork lard (forbidden to Muslims). Several soldiers based there refused to accept the cartridges; they were court-martialed and imprisoned.

The next day, the Indian troops revolted, freeing their imprisoned colleagues and killing several British officers and civilians. They then made for Delhi, where they called on the Mughal emperor, Bahadur Shah, to lead them against the British. Initially unwilling, at last he was compelled to accept. (This probably ensured that the Sikhs, who well remembered their persecution under Shah Jahan and Aurangzeb, remained on the side of the British.) The British marched on Delhi, besieging the city for nearly three months before taking it. Bahadur Shah was arrested, two of his sons and his grandson Mirza Abu Bakr were shot, and the Mughal Empire was brought to an end with Bahadur Shah's exile to Burma.

The rebellion saw a huge scale of violence and retribution. At Kanpur/Cawnpore, the British in the town were besieged for three weeks; Nana Sahib, leader of the revolt, offered General Wheeler a chance to escape by boat down the Ganges to Allahabad. The dock was surrounded by Indian troops who opened fire once most of the British had arrived. This may well have been by accident. Nana Sahib took the women and children who had survived to the Bibighar, the home of the local magistrate's clerk. However, once it was clear that the British were winning and Nana Sahib could not hold out, he ordered the massacre of all survivors. For Victorian Britons, this event symbolized the Indians' barbarity and wickedness—just like the Black Hole of Calcutta—and was used to justify reprisals.

The British eventually put down the rebellion, but the East India Company's days were numbered. The Government of India Act 1858 formally dissolved the Company and transferred its rule over India to the British government. The Company had outlasted the Mughal Empire by only a year.

Under the British Raj, Queen Victoria was installed as Empress of India, and many changes took place within India. Some of these were the disbanding of the old Bengal Army regiments and the decision to recruit primarily from among the Sikhs, Baluchis, and Gurkhas, who had either supported the British or not been involved in the revolt. Maharajas and large landholders, who had mostly refused to support the revolt, were rewarded by having their territories guaranteed; no more land reforms would be carried out for nearly a century.

The Industrial Revolution had already impacted India, but this accelerated. Railways were built throughout India, with new roads, bridges, and even canals—though these were intended to benefit the import and export trades in British control rather than Indian interests. Nonetheless, the coming of the railway created a vast infrastructure that has had a huge influence on Indian life. Many Indians migrate across the subcontinent to work in the big cities, while it's not unusual for a student to take a full-day train journey to attend one of the best-reputed universities or technical institutes. (Mahatma Gandhi always traveled third class to meet the ordinary people of India and even wrote a book entitled Third Class in Indian Railways.)

The railways also created a huge source of employment; Anglo-Indians, in particular, formed a large community of railway employees. Indian Railways now employ 1.3 million people and is introducing a new generation of super-fast trains, such as the Shatabdi Express.

CST Terminal, Mumbai—the railways in Indo-Saracenic style.
Usernamekiran, CC BY-SA 4.0 <https://creativecommons.org/licenses/by-sa/4.0>, via Wikimedia Commons; https://commons.wikimedia.org/wiki/File:Chhatrapati_Shivaji_Terminus_railway_station_(cropped).jpg

Although Indians were still second-class citizens in their own country, education opened new opportunities. By the late nineteenth century, some Indians started studying in England, often gaining legal qualifications. The fathers of Independence were mostly London-educated barristers (today, they would be more likely to have been educated at Harvard or MIT).

There is no doubt among modern historians that the Raj drained India of wealth just as effectively as the Company had done. Even John Sullivan, the Company's Collector at Coimbatore, admitted how little Company rule did for India: "The little court disappears—trade languishes—the capital decays—the people are impoverished—the Englishman flourishes, and acts like a sponge, drawing up riches from the banks of the Ganges, and squeezing them down upon the banks of the Thames" (cited in Tharoor, Inglorious Empire, Ch. 1).

In the eighteenth century, India had exported finished materials to Europe. Under the Raj, it was prevented from competing with British industry and became a provider of raw materials instead; in fact, Britain started exporting cloth *to* India. The railways imported their locomotives from Britain, and the Indian taxpayer paid for them. No wonder that by the early twentieth century, Indians were beginning to think about independence.

Chapter 6: Gandhi: Freedom and Partition

The story of Indian independence is not just the story of Gandhi, but it is impossible to imagine independence coming about the way it did without Gandhi's involvement. Gandhi is, to many, the face of independence. Every city in India has an MG road named after him, and the country's banknotes feature Gandhi's face, with his trademark round spectacles.

Gandhi shown on a 5-rupee banknote, with an Ashoka column in the bottom left corner.
Reserve Bank of India / AKS.9955, CC BY-SA 4.0 <https://creativecommons.org/licenses/by-sa/4.0>, via Wikimedia Commons; https://commons.wikimedia.org/wiki/File:5_Rupees_%28Obverse%29.jpg

Born in Porbandar, Gujarat, where his father was chief minister, Gandhi studied as a lawyer at the Inner Temple, London. Even then, his principles and his methods of social action were becoming clear: he was involved in supporting a dockers' strike and joined the London Vegetarian Society. In 1893, he moved to South Africa (another British colony), practicing law there for twenty-one years.

It was in South Africa that he saw racial discrimination first-hand. He'd considered himself "a Briton first and an Indian second" (Herman, 87). But when he moved to South Africa, he discovered that his skin made him an Indian first and was subject to many, often humiliating, restrictions.

Gandhi founded the Natal Indian Congress and began to create a coherent Indian political voice in South Africa; he also worked as ambulance corps and stretcher-bearer in the Boer War and the Zulu Revolt. In 1914, he found himself aboard a ship for London when the First World War broke out. When he arrived, he organized a volunteer ambulance corps whose members were mainly Indian students in London and took nursing classes.

In 1915, he returned to India and started working for civil rights. For instance, in 1917, he assisted peasants growing indigo in Bihar but not receiving adequate pay; he won significant concessions for them. In 1918, when Kheda was hit by floods, he organized a social boycott of tax officials using non-cooperation to achieve his arms. Eventually, the government gave way, suspending taxes for 1918 and 1919.

Gandhi often worked with the lowest classes, and his vision for independence was resolutely Indian. Earlier nationalists, for instance in Bengal, had often looked to English institutions as a way forward and got much of their support from the growing Indian middle class. Gandhi not only worked with the workers and farmers but also reclaimed Indian traditions, becoming an Indian leader visibly with his decision to wear traditional clothing rather than the western suit.

The end of the First World War brought disillusionment for many Indians. Many of the Indian regiments had fought in the war, in France or at Gallipoli, and had expected to be given increasing democracy as a result. Britain gave them nothing. In fact, they got worse than nothing, as the Rowlatt Act of 1919 was passed to block "terrorist" nationalist activities. Among other things, it allowed indefinite detention without trial.

By 1921, Gandhi had become the leader of the Indian National Congress and introduced the concept of satyagraha. His advocacy of non-violent action may seem impractical, but Gandhi considered it the only pragmatically effective way to protest. "The British want to put us on the plane of machine guns where they have the weapons and we do not. Our only assurance of beating them is putting the struggle on a plane where we have the weapons and they have not" (cited in Shirer, Ch. 1). There was nothing New Age or wishy-washy about Gandhi's tactics; he realized that the British were only able to impose the Raj through the cooperation of their Indian subjects. If the Indians stopped cooperating, British rule would—eventually—collapse.

Protest against the Rowlatt Act was particularly strong in Punjab, where General Dyer decided to impose martial law. He banned all meetings, but—most likely in ignorance rather than defiance of his edict—many villagers met in the garden of Jallianwala Bagh at Amritsar to celebrate the Sikh and Hindu festival of Vaisakhi. The crowd was estimated at about 6,000 (but may well have been more) in a park with only five entrances through narrow, lockable gates.

No order was given to the crowd to disperse. Instead, Dyer blocked the exits, then ordered his troops to fire into the garden. Firing continued for ten minutes. The number of casualties is disputed. The Times of India gave a figure of 200 killed the day after; the Hunter Commission set up by the governor-general estimated 400 deaths, including a six-week-old baby; and the Indian National Congress investigation gave a figure of 1,000 dead and 500 wounded.

Jallianwala Bagh was a turning point for many moderate Indians, including Gandhi; this appears to have been the point at which he finally lost faith in British promises of democracy within the Raj. Rabindranath Tagore, winner of the Nobel Prize for literature, renounced his British knighthood as an act of protest.

Worse, a few days later, General Dyer forced Indians in Amritsar's Kucha Kurrichhan street to crawl on their hands and knees. The "crawling order" was meant to humiliate, and it did, but it also showed many Indians that the British would never treat them as equals. Even more galling, Britain's Morning Post raised over £26,000 for Dyer's benefit.

Calls for swaraj, full independence, continued. Gandhi now advocated a policy of swadeshi, boycotting British-made goods. He clearly understood the economic underpinnings of colonialism. In 1930, he led the Salt March to Dandi, a march of 250 miles to protest the British imposition of tax on salt. He vowed that when he arrived at the sea, he would make his own salt, thus breaking the law.

At first, the action was considered by the British (and some Indians) to be a mere joke, but in fact, Gandhi had found a powerful symbol. One hundred people started the march, but thousands joined along the way. (Gandhi himself compared it to the Boston Tea Party.)

In 1931, Lord Irwin, governor-general of India, made an agreement with Gandhi to hold a Round Table Conference in London to discuss the Congress' demands. Many members of the Congress, like Jawaharlal Nehru, believed Gandhi had conceded too much. However, what the British had conceded was the principle of independence. Gandhi saw this; the British did not.

Congress' demanded the complete independence of India, with Indian control of the army, foreign policy, and economic policy; an impartial tribunal to determine the division of the national debt between India and Britain; and the right of India to secede from the British Empire at any stage.

The Round Table was packed with representatives who had been picked by the British; they made attempts to split off the Muslims, lower castes and Untouchables, and the Anglo-Indians by offering them special status. However, Gandhi made a tough and very sharp negotiator. For instance, in his argument on the division of the national debt, he asserted that British expenditure in India had been for British purposes, and therefore India should not be required to pay any of that debt. Eventually, the talks were abandoned.

While he was in Britain, Gandhi visited Lancashire mill workers, who had seen their jobs threatened as swadeshi impacted textile exports to India. They admired his grasp of the cotton business—which was not surprising since this was the main business of Ahmedabad, where he had led the first big strike against mill owners in India. Later, Gandhi told Shirer that their technology was backward; that was why they couldn't compete, and swadeshi had nothing to do with it (Shirer Ch. 11).

Throughout the 1930s, satyagraha continued. The British arrested Congress leaders and continued to try to "divide and rule," for instance suggesting separate electorates for Untouchables and Muslims. In 1935, the Government of India Act introduced a limited franchise. However, the act did not go far enough for Congress. By giving representation to Indian rulers of the princely states and giving every minority the right to vote for candidates from their own community, the act was intended to ensure that Congress could not achieve an outright majority. The act also reserved control of the Indian Army and Treasury and ensured that governors appointed by the UK retained important powers.

When the Second World War broke out in 1939, Gandhi opposed providing help to the British war effort. His point was a principled one: India, he said, could not fight a "war for democracy" while at the same time being denied its own freedom. In 1942, Gandhi launched the Quit India Movement. He was now in his seventies, but it was time, he said, to "Do or Die" (Karo ya Maro). Within hours, the leadership of Congress had been jailed without trial.

Two and a half million Indians joined the British force, nonetheless.

Perhaps this was a mistake. Congress leaders remained cooped up for most of the war, and this made it easier for Mohammed Ali Jinnah, leader of the All-India Muslim League, to secure concessions. If Congress had taken a softer line, the leaders would have kept in touch with the masses and with the British, and the arrangements made at independence might have been very different.

In February 1943, Gandhi began a fast to the death. Winston Churchill, the British prime minister and a firm opponent of Indian independence, ordered the Viceroy to let him starve; it was only owing to pressure from his Cabinet that he finally gave in. Gandhi's wife, Kasturba, died while they were still interned.

Gandhi's great failure was that he was unable to win the Muslims over. He wanted a pluralist India for Muslims and Hindus alike, but the Muslim League leadership increasingly backed a separate electorate and, in the end, a separate state. Thus, when India was finally granted independence by the Attlee government in 1947, Pakistan (including what is now Bangladesh, as East Pakistan) was separated from India.

Instead of celebrating, Gandhi spent Independence Day spinning, fasting, and praying for peace.

Gandhi's prayers were not answered. Partition led to large-scale violence between Muslims and Hindus; fifteen million people were displaced, and a million were killed. Even today, Pakistan and India have a very uneasy relationship, having fought four full-scale wars and experienced numerous border skirmishes.

Not all Hindus approved of Gandhi, either; many felt that he had been too generous to Muslims. And so, he outlived independence by just six months. On January 30, 1948, a Hindu militant, Nathuram Godse, assassinated Gandhi as he came out to address a prayer meeting.

It was the end of an era. Jawaharlal Nehru, now Prime Minister of India, addressed the country over All-India Radio:

"Friends and comrades, the light has gone out of our lives, and there is darkness everywhere, and I do not quite know what to tell you or how to say it. Our beloved leader, Bapu as we called him, the father of the nation, is no more. Perhaps I am wrong to say that; nevertheless, we will not see him again, as we have seen him for these many years, we will not run to him for advice or seek solace from him, and that is a terrible blow, not only for me, but for millions and millions in this country."

(Cited in Collins and Lapierre, Freedom at Midnight, 75.)

Chapter 7: The Indian Republic

Gandhi was instrumental in gaining independence for India and was a symbol of the struggle to find an authentically Indian existence for the nation. But he wasn't the only one working for independence, and his ideas were not shared by all his colleagues. And, of course, the idea of independence started well before Gandhi's birth—to the 1857 rebellion, in fact.

The 1857 rebellion did not start as a demand for independence but as a local mutiny. However, as the rebellion developed, it became a national revolt. For many in the independence movement, it was a defining historical moment, showing that India was capable of fighting for its rights. The later nineteenth century was a period of increasing political awareness for Indians, culminating in the foundation of the Indian National Congress in 1885.

The Indian National Congress was sparked by an idea from a Briton, retired civil servant and ornithologist Allan Octavian Hume. He believed that British rule had failed due to its contempt for Indians and aimed to create a vehicle through which Indians could express their desire for progress. At first, most of the members of Congress were made up of the western-educated elite—lawyers, journalists, and teachers—and Congress' political activity was restricted to submitting resolutions on civil rights to the Indian government, which appears not to have believed most of them worth considering. Still, Congress gave Indians a communal political voice and gave them that voice as Indians, regardless of their religion, class, caste, or place of residence.

Progress is never simple, and a huge wrench was thrown in the works by Lord Curzon, appointed viceroy of India in 1899. He was unusually sympathetic to Indian culture and the Indian people; he had traveled across Asia and the Middle East, giving him a feel for non-European societies and cultures—quite unusual in a viceroy. He restored the Taj Mahal and the tomb of Emperor Akbar at Sikandra; he also determined that crimes committed by Britons against Indians should be more severely punished. (Formerly, there was a legal double standard that punished Indians more severely than the British for crimes against members of the other race.) Curzon saw the importance of India to British economic and political power and aimed to tie the Raj even more securely to the UK.

So, it is ironic that Curzon was responsible for an act that gave new impetus to the desire for independence and also started to drive a wedge between the Muslim and Hindu independence movements. His partition of Bengal in 1905 was one of the worst things he could possibly have done.

Bengal was India's largest province by far. It included today's states of Bihar, parts of Orissa and Assam, as well as what is now Bangladesh; administering such a large state was a difficult job. Curzon's intention was simply to reduce the tasks of administration to a scale that was easier to handle, but he appears not to have really understood the political sensitivity of his decision.

By splitting the state into East and West Bengal, he was also splitting it into a Muslim-majority state and a Hindu-majority state, respectively. This reflected the "divide and rule" tactics of the Raj even if that was not his intention. He was also reducing Hindu Bengalis to a minority within West Bengal, which they had to share with Oriya and Maithili speakers. Many Hindu Bengalis—particularly the English-educated middle classes of Calcutta—saw this as an attack on their influence.

The partition of Bengal immediately triggered a nationalist reaction. In 1911, it was unwound; Bihar and Orissa became a new province, and Bengal was reunited. However, Curzon's damage could not be undone. The Muslims of East Bengal, having had their own province for six years, now felt let down, and this resentment led many Muslims toward the idea of separate electorates to safeguard their rights. Although Congress espoused the idea of a secular, multi-faith India, it was increasingly seen as a Hindu party, and the All-India Muslim League, established in Dhaka in 1906, became increasingly powerful.

Congress was largely a moderate party, espousing change within British institutions. However, a less moderate wing of the party shared the views of Congress member Bal Gangadhar Tilak, that "Swaraj [independence] is my birthright and I shall have it!" Congress eventually expelled Tilak, but his views on using boycotts to damage British rule influenced Gandhi and many others; outside Congress, his message found other listeners.

While Gandhi's place as the hero of the independence struggle gives the impression that Indian nationalism was generally pacifist, there were many Indians who did not agree. Revolutionaries such as Khudiram Bose made a number of attacks on British officers in Bengal; the paramilitary Jugantar organization, associated with the Communist Party, carried out several bomb attacks and even attempted to assassinate the viceroy during a ceremonial procession in 1912 (managing to kill his mahout, while the viceroy and his wife escaped).

As mentioned previously, the desire for independence did not prevent India from supporting Britain in the First World War. Over a million Indians served in the war effort; Sikhs and Pathans (Pashtuns) fought in Northern France. However, after the war was over, British measures to give a limited amount of local power-sharing left the Indians dissatisfied. Many Indians had believed they would receive significant progress towards independence in reward for their assistance in the war, and being given representatives whose decisions could be overruled by the viceroy was not, in their view, real democracy or independence.

So, in 1920, it was in an environment of widespread discontent that Gandhi started the non-cooperation movement. It was also under his influence that Congress moved from being an elite political club to a mass movement. Gandhi was the visionary, but he had assistance from a relatively little-known creator of independence, Vallabhbhai Patel, his "fixer." Patel was the only one of the major players who had risen from the mass of the people; he had worked in the textile mills of Ahmedabad to pay for his education, then qualified as a lawyer. He gave his successful practice up to support Gandhi in the fight against extortionate taxes at flood-hit Kheda and continued to support Gandhi's political aims thereafter. Patel was a gifted organizer, raising funds and bringing people into the party; after independence, he set up the Indian Civil Service.

Jawaharlal Nehru, a Cambridge-educated lawyer, was more Westernized in his outlook than Gandhi. He became the leader of a progressive faction of Congress in the 1920s and did not always agree with

Gandhi; in particular, he thought India should have supported the Allied war effort in 1939. Despite these disagreements, Gandhi saw Nehru as his political successor, and it was Nehru who became India's first prime minister. As PM, he promoted science and technology, setting India on the path it follows today as a regional powerhouse of technology. His speech in Congress on the day before Independence Day shows the fervor and optimism of the time:

"Long years ago we made a tryst with destiny, and now the time comes when we shall redeem our pledge, not wholly or in full measure, but very substantially. At the stroke of the midnight hour, when the world sleeps, India will awake to life and freedom. A moment comes, which comes but rarely in history, when we step out from the old to the new, when an age ends, and when the soul of a nation long suppressed finds utterance."

Perhaps the most ambiguous figure in the fight for independence is Subhas Chandra Bose, or Netaji ("Honored Leader"). Bose was Nehru's successor as Congress leader in 1938, but he was not fully in sympathy with Gandhi's ideals of nonviolence and resigned, leaving the party. Subsequently, he attempted to gain support from Nazi Germany for a Free India Legion and then joined the Japanese, creating the Indian National Army (INA). He died when his plane crashed in Taiwan in 1945; his army had already been wiped out.

Views of Bose differ. Some Hindutva nationalists have tried to claim him as a hero; other Indians are embarrassed by what they consider his betrayal of Congress ideals.

Muhammad Ali Jinnah, another London-trained lawyer, was the longtime leader of the All-India Muslim League. He was also a member of Congress until 1920 when he resigned because he could not support the satyagraha campaign. As a thoroughly Westernized individual, he was also suspicious of Gandhi's "Hindu fads" and appeal to the masses, believing the educated elite should lead India to independence.

Gradually, Jinnah came to believe that India's Muslims needed their own state to avoid becoming marginalized in a Hindu nation. He also began to rediscover his Muslim roots; the breakup of his marriage may also have made him more introspective and perhaps turned him toward a new Muslim identity. Having created the country's partition, naturally, he is not celebrated in modern India, but he is regarded as the father of modern Pakistan, of which he became the first governor-general. Like Gandhi, he did not enjoy independence for long, dying just a year after leading his country to independence.

Winston Churchill had always been an opponent of Indian independence, but the election of Clement Attlee as British Prime Minister in 1945 opened the way to swaraj. Together with the new viceroy, Admiral Lord Louis Mountbatten, he took two years to negotiate the detailed provisions for Indian independence. However, partitioning the country into largely Hindu India and mainly Muslim Pakistan was part of the agreement. Gandhi remained true to his view that India should be a single, pluralist, secular state, but Nehru and Patel disagreed. In August 1947, two separate countries were brought into being. (Pakistan was created at midnight on the 14th and India on the 15th.)

Throughout the history of the Company and the Raj, the British had employed "divide and rule tactics," which had already led to sporadic outbreaks of Hindu-Muslim violence. Hindu purity rules also created a barrier between the communities; in some villages, separate wells were provided for each religion, as high-caste Hindus would not even drink from the same water as Muslims. Partition became a bloodbath, and this led to an increased perception that Hindus were only safe with other Hindus and Muslims with other Muslims.

There were 565 officially-recognized princely states at independence, and they were given the choice of which country they would join. For a long time, the rajas and maharajas retained their privy purse payments and their luxurious lifestyles. The Nizam of Hyderabad, however, refused to join either Pakistan or India; this was a tricky situation, as he was a Muslim ruler of a majority-Hindu state, already facing the Communist-led Telangana Rebellion. In 1948, India invaded in "Operation Polo," a five-day strike that led to the resignation of the Nizam and the integration of Hyderabad into India. A further accession followed with the integration of the Kingdom of Sikkim in 1975.

The princely families continued a life of ease but little political power until 1971 when they were finally pensioned off in the 26th Amendment to the Constitution, which withdrew their recognition and privileges. (The US has had 27 amendments in over 200 years; India has already had 105 amendments since independence.)

From independence, the fortunes of Pakistan and India began to diverge. Pakistan remained a dominion of the British Empire until 1956, when it received a new constitution as an Islamic Republic, explicitly recognizing Allah's domination over the universe in its law. War with

India in 1965 started an economic downturn, and the first democratic elections in 1970 didn't bring about democracy but instead led to the war with Bangladesh (East Pakistan) when the Awami League (a secular Bengali movement) won the elections in the east.

In 1971, President Yahya Khan launched Operation Searchlight. All political and student leaders in East Pakistan were arrested, and communications were cut off. He had assumed that opposition would crumble within a week. Genocide followed, with anywhere between 300,000 and three million Bangladeshis killed and ten million fleeing to India. In the end, it was India's intervention on the side of the independence fighters that brought about the independence of Bangladesh.

From 1972 to 1977, the Oxford-educated Zulfikar Ali Bhutto led the Pakistan People's Party to power on a socialist platform. He is an ambiguous figure, secular and internationalist, but also a violator of human rights (violently suppressing separatist movements) and a populist. He allied Pakistan with China, nationalized all industries, and carried out land reforms limiting the power of wealthy landowners. He also established the Pakistani nuclear weapons program. But he failed to create strong democratic institutions, and in 1977, he was deposed and imprisoned by the man he himself had put in charge of the army, Zia ul-Haq.

Pakistan saw over a decade of military rule, together with the growth of Islamic conservatism. After Zia's death in 1988, Benazir Bhutto, Zulfikar Ali Bhutto's daughter, was elected prime minister for the People's Party. The main opposition was Nawaz Sharif's center-right coalition, which eventually won power but was then deposed in a military coup by General Pervez Musharraf. After his resignation in 2008, Pakistan returned to democracy (though without Benazir Bhutto, who had been assassinated in 2007). However, the Taliban takeover of Afghanistan increased fundamentalist terrorism within the country, and the corruption of Nawaz Sharif (exposed in the Panama Papers) has destabilized the country. Following a no-confidence motion carried against former cricketer Imran Khan, Shehbaz Sharif, a wealthy businessman and brother of Nawaz Sharif, became Prime Minister.

Meanwhile, India saw more stability, with Congress ruling the country until 1977, gradually shifting from orthodox Socialism to a more mixed neo-liberal outlook under PM Manmohan Singh (2004-2014), who carried out economic liberalization and started a decade of high growth.

Nehru led India for thirteen years until his death in 1964, with Congress winning a landslide at every election. He invested in heavy industry, receiving investment from both the West and the Communist bloc enabled by his policy of non-alignment. Lal Bahadur Shastri, the next PM, kept most of Nehru's Cabinet and policies and made Nehru's daughter, Indira Gandhi, a minister; she succeeded him on his sudden death in 1966.

Indira Gandhi would dominate most of the next twenty years of Indian politics, filling the office of prime minister—apart from three years in opposition against the Janata Party—until her assassination in 1984. Her focus was on removing poverty, notably through the Green Revolution, enabling India to achieve its aim of food security. She also nationalized banks, insurance companies, and the cotton, steel, coal, and textile industries.

Indira Gandhi in 1989.
https://commons.wikimedia.org/wiki/File:Prime_Minister_Indira_Gandhi_in_the_US.jpg

Although Mrs. Gandhi introduced a State of Emergency from 1975 to 1977, during which she effectively ruled by decree, she remained true to her father's principles of democratic rule, calling elections in 1977, which she lost to the Janata Party. (In 1979, the Janata government started to fall apart, and Gandhi regained power in 1980.) She also made English the de facto official language, refusing to make Hindi compulsory, which gained her strong support in the south and showed a true pan-Indian vision.

However, this vision was not shared by the Sikh-led Akali Dal Party, which came to power in Punjab state. Militancy grew, using the area around the Golden Temple in Amritsar as a base, and in 1983, General Atwal of the Punjab Police was shot dead as he left the temple. In June 1984, Mrs. Gandhi ordered Operation Blue Star to clear the militants out of the temple compound. It achieved this objective but at the cost of the deaths of many innocent pilgrims and extensive damage to the temple. Later that year, two of her Sikh bodyguards assassinated her in retaliation.

Indira Gandhi was succeeded by her son, Rajiv Gandhi; he, in turn, was assassinated in 1991, and after a reversal in the party's fortunes, his widow Sonia (Italian by birth) took over as leader of Congress in 1998. She won the 2004 general elections and was chosen to lead the United Progressive Alliance but chose Manmohan Singh as prime minister instead of taking the post herself. He remained in the post until 2014 and was the first Sikh PM. He had already been the finance minister during the 1990s, deregulating the "License Raj" and reducing the state's control of the economy. The economy responded well to his intervention; under his premiership, GDP grew by as much as 9 percent a year.

Singh also introduced the National Rural Health Mission of 2005, bringing decentralized health care to rural areas with over half a million local health workers, and the Right to Education Act 2009, making education free and compulsory for all children ages 6 to 14.

More recently, Congress appears to have lost its electoral appeal; the Bharatiya Janata Party's Narendra Modi has been prime minister since 2014, leading a Hindu nationalist government to victory over a Congress that was seen as corrupt and out of touch. He relied greatly on his reputation as chief minister of Gujarat, seen as a minister who brought economic growth and infrastructure development to his state. However, his party has shifted away from secularism and become more authoritarian, though India's economy has continued to grow strongly.

One new party arrived in 2012 with the foundation of the Aam Aadmi or "Common Man" party by anti-corruption campaigner Arvind Kejriwal. The party won the city of Delhi elections—Kejriwal still serves as Chief Minister of Delhi—and it is now well represented in Punjab. It has also started to win seats in Gujarat and Goa but nationally hasn't yet made a huge impact.

Chapter 8: Indian Culture

Indian life today is a strange mixture of modernity and tradition. You can walk from a sagging stall made of plastic sacking and bamboo, selling onions wholesale, and within a minute be inside a bright, modern shopping mall full of mobile phone shops. You can be twenty minutes away from a tech campus where IBM and Microsoft have offices and see a sleeping cow in the middle of the street bring traffic to a stop. Or, you can take the air-conditioned Delhi metro to a ruined medieval fort where kids are playing cricket in the dirt.

But nonetheless, India's history has left its mark on Indian culture. For instance, the idea of renunciation is still strong; people still leave their jobs and normal lives to become monks, hermits, or ascetics. Most homes have a shrine room or at least a corner where a picture of a god or the Kaaba in Mecca is taped up on the wall. And you'll still be asked to take your shoes off while visiting a temple or a home.

Family Life, Education, and Sports

Marriages are still often arranged, and in the "marriage season" (November through February), you'll frequently see a traditional bridegroom's cavalcade, often accompanied by a slightly less traditional sound system. The urban middle classes are moving away from arranged marriages, and some newspapers give a discount on classified advertisements for those looking for a partner without making any caste distinctions. (However, you'll still often find ads looking for "light-skinned" partners; this is a real mark of status in India, and skin-lightening lotions still sell well to girls looking to improve their looks.)

But gaining the in-laws' approval is still crucial for brides since they'll often move into their husband's family home. Several generations often live together, and there's a real respect for elders, who receive the care they need from their children and grandchildren.

Indian women are still struggling with the patriarchy. Some Western gender differentiations don't exist; for instance, plenty of women become engineers, and you'll also find women in road-building gangs. While many high-profile rape cases have shown the huge tension of gender relations in India (particularly as many young men can't afford to marry), things are changing. Many professional families are now settling for two daughters instead of trying for a son. Colonial-era laws criminalizing homosexuality have also been successfully challenged in the Supreme Court, and hijras (male transsexuals) were recognized officially as a third gender in 2014.

Indians have great respect for education, and one of the remaining influences of the Raj is the school uniform still worn by many Indian pupils. It is not unusual to see graduation photos even in the poorest households, as frequently parents will live frugally to ensure a good education for their children, both male and female. However, educational standards vary widely across the country. While there is almost universal literacy in Kerala, Bihar, Arunachal Pradesh, and Rajasthan still only manage 67-69 percent, and female literacy is only just over 50 percent.

Indian dress is varied. Middle-class workers will often wear Western business attire, but women will often still wear saris or a salwar suit (tunic and leggings with a matching scarf or wrap). In rural areas, local and tribal dress is often common. Muslim men may wear Western clothes or a kurta (long white shirt) with trousers.

However, religious rites sometimes have particular requirements. Some temples require men to wear a dhoti (a loincloth such as Gandhi wore), and some will not admit men who are wearing clothing on their torsos—they must be bare-chested.

India has been able to enjoy its revenge on Britain by adopting the sport of cricket and frequently beating the English at their own game. Indian children will play anywhere they can find a flat bit of ground and a stick and stone to use as a bat and ball. The Indian Premier League is now the best-attended cricket league in the world and a multi-million-dollar business; it's even broadcast live on YouTube.

Second only to cricket comes kabaddi, a traditional sport something like a game of tag in which a "raider" from one team aims to tag as many of the other team's seven members as possible without being tackled. So far, India has won every single Kabaddi World Cup, with Iran as runners-up each time.

Indian Arts

India has a rich artistic heritage. From the rock-cut temples of Ellora and Mamallapuram to the perfection of the Taj Mahal, its architecture is fascinating; even the British Raj couldn't resist Indian styles, creating what's known as the Indo-Saracenic school for public buildings such as Mumbai's CST railway terminal, the Taj Mahal hotel, and the Howrah railway station in Kolkata.

Images of the gods are often found in Indian art, both as cult statues (murti) and as figures in narrative or miniature paintings. For instance, the palace in Bundi, Rajasthan, contains rooms covered with paintings of the life of Krishna; that's also a favorite subject for Rajput miniature painters. While the Mughal court was Muslim, ruling out portrayals of deities, the painting of portraits and historical narratives was encouraged. Portraits were often highly observant and individual, including those of Hindu holy men as well as emperors and their retainers.

More recently, India has seen a rediscovery of village and tribal art traditions, such as Madhubani painting. Originally used to decorate the walls of houses, this painting has now been adapted to use on paper. Strong black ink patterns surround vivid colors, with traditional motifs such as fish, the tree of life, and the stories of Krishna and Radha.

India also has a rich tradition of decorative arts, including jewelry and textiles. Many of these are very local, such as Bandhani tie-and-dye in Gujarat and Phulkari geometrical embroidery from Punjab. Varanasi still has a silk-weaving industry, as does Chanderi, where the local prince set up a mixed cotton and silk weaving workshop to provide employment.

While some artists restrict themselves to producing traditional-style works for the tourist trade, fine contemporary art is being created, too. M. F. Husain created intensely-colored, cubist-influenced art, taking topics as diverse as folklore, religious tales, Mother Teresa, and the Raj. Though a Muslim by birth, he painted Hindu gods, too—eventually self-exiling after his naked Mother India painting got him embroiled in a culture war with Hindu right-wingers.

Prominent on the world art scene is Anish Kapoor, an artist of mixed Bombay Jewish and Hindu heritage who is now a dual British-Indian national. Kapoor's explorations of matter and void have often drawn on

Hindu symbolism. For instance, he uses holes bored in stone and filled with vivid pigments to create forms that evoke Hindu shrines and the sacred color red (for instance, the red wax in his Svayambh, which evokes blood, sacrifice, or transfiguration).

Indian music has gained many admirers in the west; sitar player Ravi Shankar played with both violinist Yehudi Menuhin and composer Philip Glass, and George Harrison of the Beatles was profoundly influenced by Shankar's playing, too. Classical Indian music is based on the idea of tala, a cyclical rhythmic structure joined with raga, a melodic framework. The raga is not just a scale, as in Western music, but includes certain motifs and evokes specific feelings. There are morning, evening, and night ragas; while some are serious and sad, others are lighthearted or joyous.

Bhajans are frequently sung in temples, and Indian Muslims have developed a similar tradition of sacred singing called Qawwali, of which the Pakistani singer Nusrat Fateh Ali Khan was the best-known performer.

In modern India, though, it's not classical or religious singers who are the best known, but "playback singers" who sing the musical numbers for actors in Bollywood films. While they may not appear on the screen, they are still celebrated, sometimes giving concerts on their own account. Asha Bhosle and Lata Mangeshkar were the two most celebrated playback singers.

Indian film has seen some major art film auteurs, such as Satyajit Ray, but its best-known product is Bollywood (a portmanteau word made from Bombay + Hollywood). Bollywood movies generally feature a lot of song and dance routines, a love interest, and a stereotyped mustache-twirling villain. Actors such as Amitabh Bachchan (who has also worked as a playback singer) are among the richest and best-known celebrities in India. (Bachchan was also a Congress MP for Allahabad for a term, gaining a commanding majority at the election.)

India also counts not just one but two "Tollywoods"—Telegu cinema in the south and the Bengali film industry based in Tollygunge, Kolkata—as well as a thriving Tamil language cinema based in Chennai. The latter created perhaps one of the oddest movies ever filmed, Guruvayur Keshavan (1977), the biography of a famed temple elephant. (Amitabh Bachchan's stint in politics was a one-off. But the 1960s film actress Jayaram Jayalalithaa became chief minister of Tamil Nadu, racking up six terms in office.)

Food and Festivals

"Indian food is spicy," people say. And that's true, but the kind of spice and the method of cooking varies from one part of the subcontinent to another.

For instance, Gujarati food is usually vegetarian and quite sweet, with the addition of a little jaggery (palm sugar) to most dishes. In Bengal, mustard is at the heart of most dishes, together with green chili; meat is commonly eaten, often marinated in yogurt and spice before cooking. Goan cuisine mixes Portuguese and Indian influences, with vinegar to give extra piquancy to meat dishes and the frequent use of pork.

While for many families, rice and dal (lentils) is a standard dish, Indian cooking can be very luxurious. For instance, the cooking of the Mughal court left its traces on the Lucknow tradition, with kebabs, meat stews, fluffy breads, and long-stewed chicken dishes with a fine blend of spices. On the opposite end of the spectrum, Indian street food includes the panipuri, a puffed-up pastry ball full of tangy beans and potatoes—or wickedly full of hot chili sauce—and bhel puri, puffed rice with tamarind chutney, fried vermicelli ("Bombay mix"), chopped onions and tomatoes, and coriander leaf.

Indian festivals are always overwhelming events. Holi celebrates the arrival of spring, and it's the festival of colors, quite literally, in which you're liable to be sprayed with bright-colored dye or powder. Most people "play Holi" with their friends and family and give no quarter. Diwali, the festival of lights, is at the other end of the year, in early autumn; it includes fireworks, gift-giving, and a lot of confectionery.

Many localities have their own festivals. The Shia Muslim rite of Muharram is celebrated in Lucknow with processions of portable shrines known as tazias, while in Kolkata, Durga Puja worships the demon-killing goddess Durga with portable shrines set up to the goddess around the city. (At the end of the festival, they're taken in procession to the river and immersed.)

Christmas is also celebrated, notably by the Christian communities of Kerala and Tamil Nadu, which hang lighted paper stars outside their houses.

One thing that belongs with every Indian festival is noise. Fireworks are a favorite, but you'll hear brass bands, drumming, and chanting, as well as amplified music. In fact, noise is a facet of Indian life that's ever-present.

The Indian Highway Code doesn't actually contain a rule that motorists must blow their horns every five seconds, but it certainly sounds like it!

Chapter 9: Influential Indians in History

History is full of influential and incredible Indians. Akbar, for instance, is an amazing character: an illiterate man who supported scholarship, a Turkic Muslim who threw his court open to every race and religion, and an extreme sports fan who rode in elephant fights for fun. This chapter will look at a few influential Indians you may not have heard of.

Mother Teresa was a different kind of amazing. In fact, she wasn't Indian by birth; she was Albanian (though she adopted Indian citizenship). She spent her novitiate in Darjeeling and taught at Loreto Convent in Kolkata until she felt the call to do something more. Leaving her order, she founded the Missionaries of Charity in 1946. She adapted the Indian sari as the dress of the order, which ran soup kitchens, homes for lepers, and hospices for those dying of tuberculosis and, later, of AIDS. The order also managed children's clinics, schools, and orphanages.

Not all Indians approve of Mother Teresa. Some feel she motivated what has been called "poverty porn," a view of India as a backward and uncaring society; others believe she imposed Christian values that were inappropriate in a Hindu culture and secular nation. However, the Catholic Church is in no doubt about her contribution: she was canonized in 2016.

A very different kind of hero was the Indian revolutionary Bhagat Singh. He was part of a growing militant movement in the 1930s, often writing for Urdu and Punjabi newspapers and for the journal of the

Workers and Peasants Party. He was a prominent member of the Hindustan Republican Association (HRA). When Lala Lajpat Rai, a prominent member of Congress and of the independence movement, was killed in a police baton charge against protesters in Lahore, the HRA vowed to avenge his death.

Singh conspired with several others to kill the Punjab superintendent of police, James Scott. Unfortunately, he mistook the target and killed a lower-ranking officer, John Saunders. Despite a police chase and a massive search operation, all the conspirators escaped Lahore. Singh cut off his hair (grown long, in Sikh style, though he was an atheist) and swapped his turban for a felt hat.

Singh later participated in the bombing of the Delhi Assembly and—with his accomplice Batukeshwar Dutt—was arrested, tried, and sentenced to life in prison. Later, the police discovered two bomb factories that had been set up by the HRA and arrested several members of the party. They realized that Singh was involved not only in the Delhi bombing but also in the murder of Saunders. Two of his accomplices in the murder plan informed on him, making the case against him watertight.

While awaiting trial, Singh led a hunger strike of Indian prisoners who claimed that they should be treated as political prisoners. Both Nehru and Jinnah showed themselves sympathetic to Singh's cause. He was so weak that, when he came to trial, he had to be carried into the courtroom on a stretcher.

Singh received the death sentence along with two of his companions despite many appeals for clemency. He remains an iconic figure for many Indians. The Indian Post Office even devoted a stamp to him in 1968, wearing his trademark hat.

Guru Nanak was the founder of the Sikh religion and the first of its ten gurus (nine of whom were human beings). The Granth Sahib, the collected scriptures, is considered the tenth guru. He was a great traveler, though some of the stories of his travels may have been exaggerated later. He made it as far as Ladakh, in the Himalayas, where he left a walking stick pushed into the ground; it is now a venerable tree, the Datun Sahib.

His teaching of one god (Ik Onkar) reflects both the monotheism of Islam and the bhakti movement's idea that everyone can have a direct experience of God without rituals or priests. There is a rather lovely story that, when he died, the Hindus and Muslims both wanted to claim his body as a relic. But, when they pulled on the sheet in which he had been shrouded, it turned out to be filled with fresh flowers.

His ideas are expressed very simply: "Vand shhako, kirat karo, naam japo," which means share, work honestly, and say God's name. Whichever gurdwara (Sikh temple) you visit and whatever your beliefs, you will be welcome to share the communal meal (langur)—a practical example of Sikh "sharing" and social service.

B.R. Ambedkar was one of the founding fathers of the Indian Republic often overlooked by the history books. Unlike most of the other men involved in the independence movement, Ambedkar was not primarily a lawyer but an economist who was educated at Columbia and the London School of Economics. (He did have legal qualifications, too.)

He was born into the Dalit (Untouchable) caste and was the first of his caste to go to Elphinstone College in Mumbai. He was chairman of the drafting committee for the Indian Constitution and ensured it was progressive—including civil liberties, rights for women, and the reservation of jobs for scheduled castes and tribes, the equivalent of affirmative action. He also argued for a separate Dalit electorate, putting him at odds with Gandhi.

B.R. Ambedkar.
https://commons.wikimedia.org/wiki/File:Dr._Bhimrao_Ambedkar.jpg

Ambedkar led satyagraha movements to gain rights for Dalits. In Mahad, he fought for the Dalits' right to draw water from the communal water tank and, at Kalaram Temple in Nashik, to allow Dalits into the temple. Throughout his career, he suffered prejudice because of his caste.

At school, he was not allowed to touch the water jug, and when he became a professor in Mumbai, his students would not share drinking water with him. His crusade was a deeply personal one.

Eventually, he converted to Buddhism alongside nearly half a million of his followers. His form of Buddhism, called Navayana, is a politically-engaged form of Buddhism THAT rejects metaphysics and mysticism in favor of the pursuit of social justice.

Women are often left out of Indian history, partly since women of the higher class among both Rajputs and Mughals lived in privacy. Wives of the Mughal emperor were often referred to by honorific court names or by their place of birth, and it was a form of praise to say that no one knew their real names. However, women have very often refused to conform to these expectations.

Velu Nachiyar (1730-1796) was a princess of Ramanathapuram who, as an only daughter, was brought up trained in combat and archery, as well as book learning. She married the king of Sivaganga, but in 1780, he was killed in a battle with the East India Company.

Velu went to Haidar Ali of Mysore, asking him for help, and obtained 5,000 soldiers as well as some heavy artillery. She devoted herself to campaigning against the Company—the first Indian queen to do so—and successfully regained her kingdom, ruling it for ten years before abdicating in favor of her daughter Vellachi. She is known as "Veeramangai," the brave woman, to Tamils.

Another famous freedom fighter was Rani Lakshmibai of Jhansi. She had married the Maharaja of Jhansi, Gangadar Rao Newalkar, in 1842, but their only son died, leaving the maharaja without an heir. They decided to adopt a boy called Anand Rao, the son of a cousin, and renamed him Damodar Rao. But on the death of the maharaja in 1853, the British applied the Doctrine of Lapse and claimed Jhansi. Lakshmibai stayed put, and for the time being, it seems the British were willing to let the matter lie.

Lakshmibai rode well and shot well; she also fenced, lifted weights, and wrestled. But she doesn't appear to have been a political mastermind—at least, it is difficult to be certain what side she was on. In 1857, when the Indian Rebellion in Meerut began, she asked the British for permission to raise forces for her own protection. However, the fort was seized by rebel Bengal infantry, who massacred the British garrison in Jhansi and extorted money from her.

She assumed command of Jhansi, but the forces of Orchha and Datia states, allied to the East India Company, decided to invade. Many of the British believed she had abetted the massacre of the British forces, so when she appealed to them for help, she got no answer. She managed to defeat the invaders on her own, and when the British turned up some time later and demanded her surrender, she defended the city bravely but unsuccessfully.

The British were already in the city when she mounted her horse Badal with her son Damodar Rao on her back and jumped from the ramparts of the fort. The horse died, but she escaped with her son, first to Kalpi and then to Gwalior. There, she fought as a sowar (cavalry officer) and was killed in the battle for the city.

Mirabai was also a princess, but her life was very different from the Rani of Jhansi's. She was born into a Rajput royal family in the sixteenth century, but little more than that is known for certain of her early life. She became a devotee of Krishna and is widely regarded as one of the great bhakti poets. Her poems address him as "the dark one" and sometimes "the mountain lifter," referring to the story that he picked up Mount Govardhan to use as an umbrella. The poems clearly show her personal devotion, representing her as Krishna's lover and servant, completely surrendered to him.

Mirabai has also become a potent symbol of feminine freedom—a woman who refused her heritage and stuck to her beliefs despite all opposition from her family. Her bhajans are still sung today.

Sarojini Naidu was another lyric poet, writing in both Persian and English and known to her contemporaries as "the Nightingale of India." But she was also one of Gandhi's colleagues, a fervent nationalist, and the only woman on the Congress Working Committee.

Naidu was educated in England, where she became a suffragette. She had a luxurious lifestyle, refusing to sit on the floor when she visited Gandhi, wear simple clothes, or eat his "disgusting" food, and yet she happily went to jail for her principles. She had to fight Gandhi for the right to go on the Salt March—he thought it would be too tough for women—but after his arrest, Gandhi told her to take over from him as leader of the campaign.

Following independence, Naidu was appointed governor of Uttar Pradesh, the first woman to fill this office.

Gulbadan was the daughter of the Mughal emperor Babur, sister of Humayun, and much-loved aunt of Akbar. When she was 65, Akbar asked her to write an account of Humayun's life, and it is through her writings that we know the world of the royal Mughal women. She describes Hamida Banu Begum, Akbar's mother and a huge influence on the emperor; she records the way women reacted to the world around them and the way the harem exerted influence on diplomatic affairs. Her book is a counterpart to Abu'l-Fazl's account of Akbar's reign; it shows a mirror image of the male court, one that is made up of women.

Gulbadan seems to have been a strong character. She decided to make the pilgrimage to Mecca and led a woman-only hajj which took her seven years. She stayed in Mecca for four years and was shipwrecked on the Yemeni coast on her way back. When she died at the age of eighty, Akbar grieved for her as he seems to have done for no one other than his father.

Mary Kom would probably love the Rani of Jhansi and Velu Nachiyar if they were able to meet up. Mangte Chungneijang Mary Kom, to give her full name, was born in a poor Christian tribal family in the state of Manipur in northeast India. She started as a keen athlete, running and throwing javelin, but decided to take up boxing when she was 15, keeping it secret from her father. He didn't find out until she won the state boxing championship.

Her titles include six gold medals in the World Amateur Boxing Championships and a bronze medal in the 2012 Olympics. She's also the mother of three sons, and in 2018, she and her husband adopted a daughter and found time to sit in the Rajya Sabha (Senate) for six years.

Chapter 10: Buddhism vs Hinduism

India is the cradle of three faiths: Hinduism, Buddhism, and Jainism. But their three fates were very different. Hinduism, though exported to Southeast Asia early on, is now the main religion only in India (and, in a rather different form, in Bali). Buddhism made its way to Sri Lanka, Southeast Asia, and China, and through China to Korea and Japan; another form of Buddhism made its way to Tibet and Mongolia, but the faith practically died out in India after the medieval era.

The Jain religion, on the other hand, remained in India. But, unlike Buddhism, it did not proselytize actively outside the subcontinent. Today, there is a large Jain community in the states of Maharashtra, Rajasthan, Karnataka, and Gujarat, particularly in Mumbai, but overall, it is a small minority making up less than half a percent of the total population. It is, by the way, the minority with the highest rate of literacy by far and a wealthy community involved in commerce and finance.

Hinduism is a religion that is quite literally rooted in the landscape of India, from the sites of Krishna's childhood around Vrindavan and Mathura or his kingdom in Dwarka to individual sacred stones and trees. The rivers, in particular, are considered sacred; many temples have sculptures of the Ganges and Yamuna personified as goddesses guarding the door to the inner sanctuary.

Sometimes, the sacred landscape is recreated. For instance, at Mount Abu, at the foot of the Gangotri Glacier in the Himalayas, there is a holy spring called Gaumukh that is channeled into a tank through a cow's head spout; it is considered the source of the Ganges. The most widespread example of this is the way temples evoke Mount Meru in the Himalayas, Shiva's home, and the center of the universe, both through the spire of the temple representing the mountain and the windowless interior garbhagriha sanctuary representing the cave in which he practiced his austerities.

Buddhism doesn't have this kind of attachment to the landscape, though the sites of Buddha's birth, enlightenment, first sermon, and death are now pilgrimage sites attracting visitors from all over the Buddhist world. Perhaps this freed the religion to expand to other countries in a way that Hinduism found more difficult. (Even now, orthodox Hindus consider leaving India an impurity. A monk who had traveled to the US and Europe found that conservative priests wanted to ban him from becoming the head of a temple. Gandhi was excommunicated by the Bania caste when he went to London to study law and remained an out-caste for the rest of his life.)

Right from the beginning, Hindu thinkers appear to have been concerned with the question of where things came from, with the existence of emptiness and void. The Rig Veda asks questions about creation rather than telling a creation myth:

1. THEN was not non-existent nor existent: there was no realm of air, no sky beyond it.

    What covered in, and where? and what gave shelter? Was water there, unfathomed depth of water?

2. Death was not then, nor was there aught immortal: no sign was there, the day's and night's divider.

    That One Thing, breathless, breathed by its own nature: apart from it was nothing whatsoever.

3. Darkness there was: at first concealed in darkness this All was indiscriminate chaos.

    All that existed then was void and formless: by the great power of Warmth was born that Unit.

4. Thereafter rose Desire in the beginning, Desire, the primal seed and germ of Spirit.

    Sages who searched with their heart's thought discovered the existent's kinship in the non-existent.

5. Transversely was their severing line extended: what was above it then, and what below it?

There were begetters, there were mighty forces, free action here and energy up yonder

6. Who verily knows and who can here declare it, whence it was born and whence comes this creation?

The Gods are later than this world's production. Who knows then whence it first came into being?

7. He, the first origin of this creation, whether he formed it all or did not form it, Whose eye controls this world in highest heaven, he verily knows it, or perhaps he knows not.

(Rig Veda 10.129)

This concern with the nature of reality gives rise to the idea of cycles of time in which the universe is created and destroyed over and over. The idea of Brahma, Shiva, and Vishnu as a kind of "trinity" of gods is most likely a Victorian interpolation, but the dynamic of creation, preservation, and destruction is authentically Hindu.

Buddhism, too, has this dizzying idea of a void at the center of things. The world is made up of illusions; human life is an illusion. Nirvana, like the Hindu moksha, is a salvation that is represented as release from the multiplicity and illusive nature of the physical world. The cycle of times, too, finds its place in Buddhism, with the concept of different universes and different eras.

The ideas of reincarnation and karma are found in both religions, stemming from the idea of cyclicality. Karma is seen as a natural law, the way things work; each action brings about its consequences. However, there is no idea of reward or punishment associated with it, as there is with Christian or Muslim ideas of heaven and hell; karma is simply the way things balance.

Spiritual practices are also in many ways common between Buddhism and Hinduism. Both religions use forms of yoga and meditation to liberate the soul from distraction by the illusory world; both use mantras, sacred chants, as a part of ritual and meditation. Om, or Aum, the sacred seed-syllable, is seen as the vibration from which the world arises; it invokes the single reality behind the illusory world of appearances. Common mantras include the name of a god: Om Namah Shivaya, honoring Shiva, or Hare Krishna Hare Rama. In Buddhism, one of the earliest mantras is Namo

Buddhaya, "homage to the Buddha."

Although some authorities attempt to define Hinduism as polytheistic and Buddhism as monotheistic, once you start looking in detail at the philosophies involved, there is a certain fluidity about both Hinduism and Buddhism. For instance, many Shaivites will tell you that they believe all gods are one; Mahayana Buddhists, one of the two different schools that evolved over the centuries, have many different Buddhas and bodhisattvas but will tell you that these, too, are only illusions made to bring you closer to the truth.

This fluidity is built into the idea of Brahman and Atman, the world soul and the individual soul. The individual soul can commune and even fuse with the world soul, becoming absorbed in it. In bhakti, devotees achieve complete immersion in their god: some sources tell of Mirabai being absorbed physically into a statue of Lord Krishna.

Men and gods overlap. Vishnu has several incarnations, or avatars, including Krishna, Rama, and the Buddha. At the Mahabodhi Temple in Bodh Gaya, the site of Buddha's enlightenment, most of the pilgrims are Buddhists, but there are always a few Hindu holy men with long white beards and hair and bright yellow robes, worshiping Vishnu in the avatar of Buddha. In Tibetan Buddhism, on the other hand, some Hindu gods find themselves transformed into Buddhist deities, such as Ganesh, who becomes Ganapati, and the jolly little god of wealth, Jambhala—but they are only subsidiary figures, subservient to the Buddhas.

This kind of fluidity is also typical of Indian art and architecture. For instance, many temples are made up of repeated motifs which turn out to be practically miniature temples. In Mughal times, a particularly delightful artistic endeavor was making up elephants or swans out of other animals or human bodies—which is real, the elephant or the human figures? There's no easy answer.

India has had a literate culture since the first millennium. Inscriptions are everywhere: there are written land grants, the Ashoka pillars, mantras, and Persian calligraphy. But unlike Judeo-Christian religions, neither Hinduism nor Buddhism has a single sacred text—they have a corpus of texts of differing authority. For instance, a Krishna devotee might read the Bhagavad Gita as their only guide, going deeper and deeper into its meanings as they re-read it again and again, even though it's just a small part of the larger Mahabharata.

In Buddhism, too, there is no one text that stands above all. Buddhism has a concept of skillful means (upaya), that is, the way that the Buddha's message can be tailored for each individual to help them towards enlightenment. That might be the Tripitaka (Buddha's teachings as written down by those who heard him or received them through the oral tradition), but it might include the Jataka tales of Buddha's earlier lives or the Tantric texts that emerged later. In one sermon, Buddha simply held up a flower, and his student Mahakasyapa became enlightened simply by seeing it.

Why did Buddhism leave India while Hinduism remained strong? After the end of the Gupta Empire, Buddhism seems to have lost most of its patronage from royal sources. Perhaps one of the reasons is that Hinduism changed, with devotional movements offering individuals a more meaningful and personal relationship with the gods. The Buddhists and Jains had challenged ritual Hinduism and the caste system; bhakti, which did not allow caste to come between the worshiper and their god, made up for what had been missing in Hinduism.

Another possible reason is that Buddhism became a monastic religion, and the large Buddhist monasteries became divorced from day-to-day life; Buddhism didn't offer much advice for lay people. (This is something the Jains certainly did offer, with a huge amount of advice on how to live well in an ordinary family.) On the other hand, Hinduism offered a range of different ways for the individual to be involved in religion, whether through rites of puja, singing bhajans, making pilgrimages, or living the life of a renunciate yogi.

At the same time, when the Turks invaded through Afghanistan, the fact that Buddhism had spread to other countries made it easier for monks to migrate to the Himalayas, China, Sri Lanka, and Southeast Asia. Once Buddhist monasteries had been sacked, the Sangha died out as its leaders fled. Since most of the large Buddhist centers were in northern India, they experienced the brunt of early invasions. Hindus, on the contrary, were well represented in southern India, which could resist invasion.

It is also worth considering that Buddhism did not need India in the same way that Hinduism did. It did not rely on a sacred landscape, and its more thorough-going dismissal of the world as illusory meant it was not tied to sacred sites in the same way as Hinduism. On the other hand, Hindu movements such as bhakti intensified the presence of Hinduism in the landscape, for instance with Chaitanya's rediscovery of the land of Braj and the landscape of Krishna's birth and early life around Vrindavan and Mathura.

Conclusion

The Republic of India is now three-quarters of a century old. India itself is several millennia older.

But the Republic still has some unfinished business. There are still hard feelings about colonialism, which came to the fore recently with the accession of King Charles III. Indians fretted about whether the queen consort would wear a crown including the famous Koh-i-Noor diamond that once belonged to the Sikh Empire—and possibly, before that, to Shah Jahan as part of his Peacock Throne. (She won't.)

There are also still hard feelings about partition. Pakistan and India have had four wars and numerous skirmishes and are still in conflict. Bangladesh, on the other hand, has begun to establish a positive relationship with India. However, Narendra Modi's espousal of Hindutva and anti-Muslim rhetoric make it hard to see India becoming fully reconciled with its Muslim neighbors.

It's still a challenge to bring poorer states like Bihar and Rajasthan up to the status of wealthier states like Gujarat and Kerala. Literacy rates, economic production, and wealth vary very greatly between states, hence the presence of many migrant workers from poorer states in Delhi and other big cities.

But India is definitely reaching for the future. Young Indians are often fearsomely well-educated, particularly in scientific and technological subjects; India has a huge high-tech economy. Everyone is on WhatsApp and Facebook, even in small villages, and India has now become the world's fastest-growing mobile payments market. Because English is widely spoken, the country has become home to numerous call centers, technical support centers, and software outsourcing businesses.

Economically, India has been shadowed by China. But a lot of China's recent progress has been driven by high indebtedness, and Chinese companies are not noted for their quality. Besides, Chinese businesses are controlled by the state. In India, on the other hand, anyone can set up a business; the cost of entry is low, and deregulation has removed many of the License Raj's roadblocks. The future is full of opportunity.

India's future? The Indian School of Business campus in Mohali.
MBAaspire11, CC BY-SA 3.0 <https://creativecommons.org/licenses/by-sa/3.0>, via Wikimedia Commons. https://en.wikipedia.org/wiki/File:ISB%27s_Mohali_Campus.jpg

Yet India retains its distinctive culture in a modern world. For instance, traditional Ayurvedic medicine is now researched in a scientific way and taught as an option in medical schools to students who have already learned Western sciences and anatomy. Tea stands and falooda parlous still outnumber McDonald's. And depending on the city, you may still be woken in the early morning by the muezzin or the sound of loudspeakers broadcasting "Om Nama Shivaya" from the local temple.

India might become the "silicon subcontinent." It might take the world of renewable energy by storm. But whatever happens, it's never going to be quite like anywhere else.

Dates

2600-1700 BCE	Harappan civilization
1500-500 BCE	Compilation of the Vedas
6th century BCE	Early states in Indo-Gangetic Plain: Mahavira, Buddha
327-5 BCE	Alexander the Great in India
321 BCE	Chandragupta founds the Mauryan dynasty
268 BCE	Ashoka accedes to the throne
185 BCE	End of Mauryan rule
180-65 BCE	Rule of Menander: Indo-Greek dynasty in NW
1st century CE	Kushan state founded
320	Accession of Chandragupta, founder of Gupta dynasty
410	Visit of Fa Hsien, "Monkey"
c. 550	Chalukya dynasty begins, Badami

c. 570	Pallava rule in Kanchi
712	Arab conquest of Sind
752	Rashtrakutas beat Chalukyas
770	Pala dynasty, eastern India
c. 900	Chola become powerful, South India
973	Chalukyas defeat Rashtrakutas
1075	Ramanuja
1110	Rise of the Hoysala dynasty
1192	Battle of Tarain, Muhammad Ghuri defeats Chauhan
1206	Establishment of Delhi sultanate
1279	End of Chola power
1398	Timur sacks Delhi
1526	First Battle of Panipat, at which Babur defeats the Lodi sultanate of Delhi
1540	Sher Shah Suri establishes the Sur Empire after conquering Humayun
1555	Humayun reconquers Hindustan
1556	Accession of Akbar: Second battle of Panipat, Mughals defeat Afghans
1562	Akbar abolishes jizya tax on non-Muslims
1572	Akbar takes Ahmedabad, Gujarat
1574	Akbar takes Patna

1600	Foundation of East India Company
1739	Persians sack Delhi
1751	Robert Clive seizes Arcot
1757	British defeat Siraj ud-Daulah in Bengal
1784	India Act brings the EIC under government control.
1799	Tipu Sultan of Mysore killed in battle, British take Seringapatam
1843	British capture Sind: doctrine of lapse
1853	Railway built from Thane to Bombay—first in India
1857	Sepoy Mutiny/First War of Independence
1876	Queen Victoria proclaimed Empress of India
1911	Delhi becomes capital
1919	Jallianwala Bagh massacre, Amritsar
1930	The Salt March
1947	Independence, Partition of India
1975	Sikkim incorporated into India

Glossary

Ahimsa - nonviolence, a central tenet of Buddhist and Jain faiths.

Ashram - a hermitage or religious community.

Bhajan - a devotional song (Hindu).

Bhakti - a movement which espouses gaining salvation through intense personal devotion to a god.

Bharat - India (as in Mahabharata).

Chaitya - Buddhist place of worship.

Chakravartin – "world-ruler," the ideal universal ruler; applied to rulers whose empire includes previously separate kingdoms, or is of great extent (e.g., Ashoka).

Darshan – "viewing" of an idol, a religious experience which bestows blessings on the worshiper.

Dhoti - loincloth.

Factory - in its original sense, a trading post through which a foreign power was able to channel its trade with India.

Gana-sangha - rule by tribal assembly, in which a king (raja) governed with the assistance of the assembly.

Gopura - a tower gateway (Southern India).

Hajj - the Muslim pilgrimage to Mecca.

Hindutva - an ideology which sees India as essentially (and potentially, exclusively) Hindu, espoused by the right wing and by the BJP Party.

Jagir - a district whose tax revenues were assigned to a holder, the jagirdar, under Mughal administration.

Jauhar - self-immolation when it was obvious that a fort was going to be taken. The women would usually burn themselves and the men would go on a suicidal sortie against the enemy.

Jizya - special tax on non-Muslims.

Mandapa - a pillared hall for public rituals, often attached to the sanctuary of a temple but sometimes separate.

Mandir - a temple.

Mansab - a military pay grade in the Mughal empire, held by a mansabdar.

Matha or mutt - a Hindu monastery.

Moksha - salvation (for Hindus): a similar concept to Buddhist nirvana.

Puja - worshiping a deity by giving it food, incense, etc.

Qawwali - a form of Muslim devotional song.

Raga - a basic musical mode, including a scale and certain melodic motifs.

Raj – "rule"; British Raj, the period of direct British rule of India from 1858 to 1947.

Raja, maharaja - ruler, great ruler: title of Indian kings.

Sallekhana - the Jain vow of fasting to the death; gradual reduction of food intake.

Sangha - community; specifically, the Buddhist monastic community.

Sari or saree - form of dress for Indian women consisting of a single draped piece of cloth.

Sati or suttee - immolation of a widow on the funeral pyre of her dead husband: now criminalized.

Satyagraha - non-violent protest or civil disobedience.

Sepoy - an Indian soldier.

Shaivite - any sect or person devoted to the God Shiva.

Shikara - spire of a northern style Indian temple.

Sowar - an Indian horseback warrior.

Stupa - a mound erected to enclose Buddhist relics.

Swadeshi – "made in India"; the movement to boycott British imports and use only Indian materials and products.

Swaraj - independence.

Vaishnavite - person or sect devoted to the God Vishnu.
Vihara - a Buddhist monastery.
Vimana - spire of a southern style Indian temple.
Zamindar - a landowner who leases his land to tenant farmers.

Part 2: Indian Mythology

An Enthralling Overview of Myths, Gods, and Goddesses from India

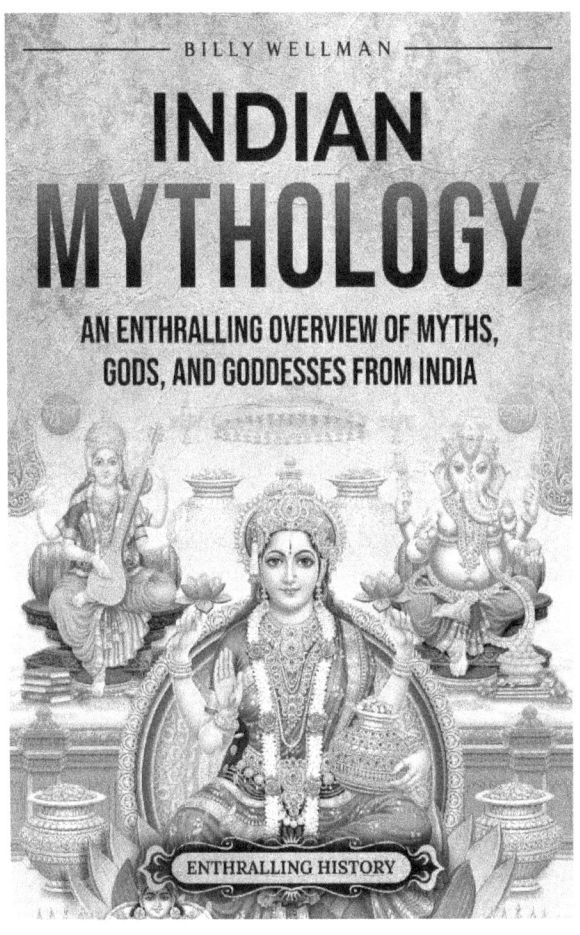

Introduction

A perusal of ancient Indian texts reveals intricately woven mythical tales, largely emerging from and influencing religion. Much of Indian mythology centers around the tales of gods and goddesses, the stories of sacred deities, and legends that are interconnected with forces of nature and form significant aspects of the world and life on earth.

Indian mythology largely originates from ancient texts like the Puranas, the Vedas, the *Mahabharata*, and the *Ramayana*. These texts deal with the understanding of life, gods, and creation, acting as a guide into the life of earlier civilizations. In addition to dealing with the spiritual and the religious, these ancient texts also deal with other aspects of living, such as medicine, music, and mantras.

This book is designed to provide a comprehensive understanding of Indian mythology, its various traditions and philosophies, and the ways in which it has created and sustained religious beliefs. In addition to covering the creation of the world, the book also discusses in detail the various deities that play a significant role in Indian mythology and how they contribute to the understanding of the world from a Hindu perspective. It also covers some of the most common tales and legends found in Indian mythology.

The detailed discussion of Indian mythology in this book should help you understand its importance and what beliefs, myths, and legends act as its central basis. Uncover stories that provide insight into everyday life (yes, even today!) and spirituality. We encourage you to form your own conclusions about how these stories might impact people's understanding of the world.

Chapter 1: The Hindu Cosmos

Stories of creation in Indian mythology are categorized under Hindu cosmology and do not originate from any single source. Rather, there are multiple overlapping accounts of how the world came to be. Various texts provide different answers to the question of creation, citing the role of different spiritual forces and deities in creating and maintaining order and balance in the universe.

While the stories of creation in Hindu mythology are interconnected, they are also, in some instances, contradictory. There is no unified basis for Hindu beliefs, and each text may present a wholly different view of the origins of life. Regardless, these beliefs formulate a core aspect of Hinduism, and their contradictory nature may be due to the fact that these mythological accounts were developed at different periods to answer different questions regarding the world's existence.

Creation in the Vedas

The four Vedas, which comprise thousands of texts, each deal with different aspects of life, creation, spirituality, and worship. One of these books is the Rig Veda, the earliest of the ancient Indian texts. Each of the Vedas also includes four key sections, of which the late Vedic Upanishad texts (the most recent addition to the Vedas) deal with philosophical understanding and spirituality.

The Rig Veda

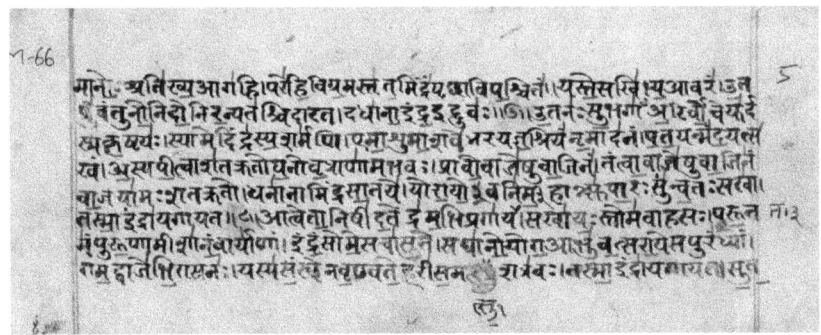

Part of the Rig Veda manuscript.
Ms Sarah Welch, CC BY-SA 4.0 <https://creativecommons.org/licenses/by-sa/4.0>, via Wikimedia Commons; https://commons.wikimedia.org/wiki/File:1500-1200_BCE_Rigveda,_manuscript_page_sample_ii,_Sanskrit,_Devanagari.jpg

The Rig Veda comprises over one thousand hymns in praise of the gods, most prominently Indra. The hymns also deal with the subject of creation. Many of these hymns are still recited during various Hindu festivals. The Rig Veda was originally written in ancient Vedic, which eventually transformed into Sanskrit, and speaks of the life of the Indo-Aryan people in the Vedic age, especially in relation to their questions of philosophy and creation.

Much of the text within the Rig Veda makes use of symbolism and allegory, leaving the text open to interpretation and producing conflicting accounts of the universe's creation.

For example, the Purusha Sukta, a hymn in the Rig Veda, identifies the origins of creation emerging from the destruction of Purusha. Purusha is described as the cosmic being who has always been there and will always be there—an indestructible and eternal universal principle. This being sacrificed itself, and from its body emerged the four kinds of people—the Rajanya, the Brahmin, the Shudra, and the Vaishya.

Another story of creation is the mundane egg or cosmic egg, which forms the physical world around us and was separated into the male-female energy from which life on earth was created. Other creations were also brought into the world, including everything from air and fire to people, the universe, and the gods Agni and Indra.

Upanishads

The Upanishads emerged in the late Vedic period, and they are concerned with understanding the relationship between cosmic powers and humans. The Upanishads talk about the "Self," Atman, which is all that existed in the beginning. While Atman can be understood to mean the soul, it is more aptly translated as the "Self," denoting consciousness, which is the essence of being alive. From the Self emerged the earth and the sky, as well as heaven and hell, which are temporary abodes of rebirth.

The overlapping nature of mythology can be seen in the Upanishads' narration of creation. According to these texts, Purusha existed only as Atman in the beginning and later divided himself into two, male and female, on account of loneliness. Existence then came in pairs. The male embraced the female, and the female, becoming a cow, was embraced by the male as a bull, as well as other animals, such as horses and sheep. Later, the gods and their powers were created, as well as fire and the principles of righteousness.

In essence, the Upanishads show the Self as the beginning of all creation, a non-being from which beings emerged. Since Purusha developed from the Self, he is the beginning of the creation of the world, and by him, life is sustained.

Hiranyagarbha Sukta

Hiranyagarbha Sukta is a hymn in the Rig Veda that talks about the "golden egg" or the cosmic egg, which is thought to be the source of the creation of the universe, existing before creation itself. How this egg came to be the source of creation is a subject of debate. One interpretation of the text suggests that Purusha fertilized an embryo with the natural force, Prakrti, from which the world was created.

Other interpretations view the egg as the source of creation, as the god Brahma emerged from this egg and created the universe and everything in it. Some also suggest that Brahma may have been the egg. Much like the Self, the egg existed before anything else, a non-being from which other beings emerged. While it may be the source of creation according to some texts, the way it created life as we know it is open to interpretation.

Brahmana

The Brahmana texts within the Vedas offer an explanation of the hymns contained in these works and, as such, offer a story on the creation of the world. This story centers around Prajapati, who is the major deity of creation from the Vedic period. While Prajapati has been used to denote various deities in the earlier texts, later Vedic texts refer to him as a single deity and the lord of creation. He is often identified with the Hindu god

Brahma.

Prajapati is said to have undergone Tapas, or asceticism, to reproduce with a female partner, sometimes stated to be Vac and other times Ushas. From the first primal water came the golden egg, from which emerged Prajapati. He then created the universe, including everything in it, as well as the Devas (the cosmic deities) and the demigods or Asuras, who, according to some sources, brought about darkness.

The Brahmana speaks of a single line of descent, much like other major religions of the world, like Christianity and Islam, which suggest that the human race is descended from Adam. The Brahmana also describes a great flood that wiped out the human race, leaving only Manu, the last of men. From his sacrifice, the goddess Ida was born, and with her power, the entirety of the current human generation is descended from him.

The Question of Creation: Nasadiya Sukta

Not all texts within the Rig Veda seek to answer the question of the source of creation. Since the texts also deal with philosophical inquiries, the Nasadiya Sukta, known as the Hymn of Creation, poses questions about what led to the creation of the universe rather than seeking to answer them.

This text suggests that any gods credited with the creation of the universe did not exist before it but rather came into existence after the universe was created, leaving the question as to how the world came into being with no gods to create it. The text does not offer any answers or explanations and suggests it may be a truth that can never be known.

Creation in the Puranas

The oldest of the Puranic texts date back to between the 3rd and the 8th century CE. The Puranas deal with the questions of cosmology and establishing the origins of various gods. Many of the books within the Puranic texts are named after gods, discussing where they come from and the role they play in creating and sustaining life. Therefore, the Puranas offer a variety of myths, each offering different explanations of the creation of the world.

Some texts in the Puranas attribute the creation of the world to the god Brahma, tying in the concept of the golden egg, which he may have embodied or from which he may have emerged. Other texts depict a more hierarchical structure of creation emerging from nothing but Brahma, the ultimate universal truth and cause for creation. In other stories, Vishnu, who is part of the Trimurti, is seen as the source of creation. According to these stories, Vishnu created the four-faced god called Brahma. Vishnu's incarnation on earth, Rama, which emerged from a fire sacrifice, is one of the most famous and worshiped incarnations of Vishnu.

Brahma proceeded to create aspects of the universe, including various divine beings and creatures that emerged from parts of his body, such as snakes from his hair and cows from his stomach. The people of the Vedic period came from his body parts and four mouths. Brahma also created a lineage. His wives went on to give birth to other celestial beings and all of creation, including animals and plants.

Brahmanda

The Brahmanda Purana is one of the major Puranic texts. Brahmanda itself refers to the cosmic egg. The text explains the formation of the universe, suggesting that Brahma created and divided the universe into three parts, which were later further broken up into fourteen parts. These realms denote the multi-layered nature of the universe, with some grouped together to create heaven, hell, and earth in a single universe.

The creations that came later, that of living beings and the elements of the earth, were to populate these realms. Some Puranas have suggested the existence of multiple universes, though all of them were created, populated, and destroyed by Brahma. The mythological accounts of the Brahmanda also provide depictions of what the universe looks like, including the radius of the universe and the size and composition of its various elements, such as the stars, the sun, and the moon.

Facets of the Mythology of Creation

The issues of creation within Indian mythology are not limited to simply explaining how the universe came to be. While much of it discusses the role of gods and various deities, mythological texts also explain what these creations were. The ideas of time, matter, and life, which make up the world, are discussed in these texts as well.

Matter

The Vedas, in particular, talk about the elements of matter in the universe. All matter is believed to have three essential qualities or *gunas*:

- Good (*sattva*)
- Darkness or ignorance (*tamas*)
- Passion (*rajas*)

Matter is created when the three qualities are in three possible states. Root matter, Pradhana, occurs in a state of equilibrium when the qualities remain unmixed and unmanifested, that is to say when the three qualities have not interacted with each other to create other matter. Primal matter, or Prakrti, occurs when the *gunas* are mixed but not manifested, creating a state of agitation when interaction has occurred but nothing else has been created. Finally, matter, Mahat-tattva, is created when *gunas* are mixed and manifested into new matter.

Root matter, or Pradhana, cannot act on its own, as the *gunas* within it exist in an unmanifested state. Thus, it lacks consciousness until agitated by a primal desire to create something. Texts do not elaborate on where this desire may emerge from or how the *gunas* interact to supplement creation.

The matter that is finally manifested, Mahat-tattva, ranges from spiritual to individual forms of existence, leading to the creation of intangible elements, such as personality, intelligence, and the mind, and the creation of physical elements, such as space, fire, air, water, and earth, which correspond to the senses and organs created in the human body. Space relates to the experience of sound, fire to the eye, the air to the skin, the tongue to the water, and the nose to the earth.

Time

In Indian mythology, time is cyclic and infinite. Each passing universe will be replaced by other universes in a continuous loop, invariably rendering the question of the source of existence redundant. The creation and the states of matter that make up the universe are guided by time, *kala*, which stretches from the conception of the universe to its destruction, keeping the cycle going for eternity.

The Puranas, the *Mahabharata*, and the *Manusmriti* all speak of an infinite loop of time and are often denoted in terms of the *yuga*, a period of time, and, more noticeably in later texts, as *kalpa*, a day of Brahma. The process of Prakrti, for example, occurs in the span of one Brahma life, a *maha-kalpa*, amounting to over three hundred trillion years. Its matter is destroyed over an equal period of time.

A *kalpa* is over four billion years, the same amount of time it takes for matter to manifest, during which the entire process of creation and destruction takes place, starting over with the next *kalpa*. The partial destruction of matter occurs during the *pralaya*, the night of Brahma, equal in length to a day of Brahma. Each *kalpa* contains one thousand *maha-yugas*, each lasting over four million years and divided into four distinct ages: Satya, Treta, Dvapara, and Kali. Kali is the present time and is seen as a time of wickedness and chaos.

Life

The *jiva-atma* (also called *jiva*), the embodied soul that occupies a temporary home in the human body, is not itself temporary but eternal. It is believed to be neither created nor destroyed. Once manifested, each *jiva* is covered by a *guna* in a distinct manner, which allows various matter to interact with one another. For example, a conscious being, such as a human, interacts with an unconscious matter, such as the mind, which has no physical manifestation.

The material world is *maya*, non-eternal and temporary, existing in states of manifestation and non-manifestation. That is to say that the world simultaneously existed in a physical form for the people who lived on it and as non-physical matter. As such, it is considered a non-reality to the extent that it may be more akin to virtual reality, something that only exists for the people who experience it. *Maya* is denoted by the interaction between *jiva* and temporary objects. A *jiva* begins to identify with its temporary material body through material interactions, entering a state of nescience or ignorance.

Liberation, or *moksha*, for a *jiva* is achieved with self-realization, or *atman-jnana*, leading to the awareness of the true spiritual and eternal identity of the *jiva*. Hindu practice believes the observance of the righteous path, dharma, is essential to achieve *moksha*, which is important to unleash the positive qualities contained in the *jiva*, which are hidden by the *maya*.

The Multiverse

Krishna.
Sujit kumar, CC BY-SA 3.0 <https://creativecommons.org/licenses/by-sa/3.0>, via Wikimedia Commons; https://commons.wikimedia.org/wiki/File:Lord_Krishna.jpg

As the Brahmanda texts indicate, Brahma created multiple universes, each populated with its own creations. The nature of time, as explained within Indian mythology, is such that each of these universes is created and destroyed within a *kalpa*, and many of these universes exist at the same time in fourteen *lokas*, or realms.

The multiverse theory within Hindu mythology speaks of these universes existing at the same time independent of each other. Each universe is ruled by the trinity of the three primary gods: Vishnu, Brahma, and Shiva. Various Puranic and other texts explain the nature of these universes, indicating that each contains the seven elements of earth, fire, water, sky, air, energy, and ego. These universes are also limitless, moving like "atoms" in the grand scheme of creation.

The cyclic nature of time guides the creation, destruction, and re-creation of the universes within the multiverse. Each multiverse dissolves within a *maha-kalpa*, only for the process of creation to begin anew. Another multiverse then emerges, just as large and innumerable as the one before it. Seven higher and seven lower *lokas* exist in each multiverse, although this idea varies depending on the source. Different texts offer different ideas about the multiverse theory.

Chapter 2: Vishnu and His Many Avatars

One of Hinduism's main deities is Vishnu, who is known to be the cosmic guardian and preserver. He is typically depicted as a blue-skinned man with four arms holding items in his hands, usually a conch shell, discus, lotus flower, and mace. The numerous avatars or incarnations that Vishnu has undergone, which are said to be earthly representations of his holy essence, are what distinguish him from other Hindu gods. Hindu mythology holds that Vishnu embraced ten significant avatars, collectively referred to as the Dashavatara, to reestablish harmony and order in the cosmos.

Some of the most fascinating and well-liked myths in Hinduism are those about Vishnu's avatars. Every avatar, from Rama to Krishna, possesses a distinct personality and serves a particular role. For instance, Krishna is viewed as a lovely and mischievous god who epitomizes love and devotion, while Rama is venerated as the ideal monarch and the personification of righteousness.

One interesting thing to note here is that Hinduism is not the only religion in which Vishnu manifests. The legends of Vishnu's avatars have been adopted into a variety of Southeast Asian cultures, including the Javanese and the Balinese. There are several representations of Vishnu's avatars throughout the Angkor Wat temple complex in Cambodia, the biggest religious structure in the world.

We will delve into the intriguing world of Vishnu and his numerous avatars in this chapter. As we explore the tales and legends that surround each avatar, we'll look at their origins, meanings, and symbols. We'll also look at how the idea of an avatar has changed through time, from its roots in ancient Hindu mythology to its contemporary cultural and artistic manifestations.

The Pervader: Lord Vishnu

In Hinduism, Lord Vishnu is worshiped as the defender and preserver of the cosmos. He is known to be one of the main gods. Vishnu is known by various names, one of which is "the Pervader," a reference to his power to express himself in all things and beings in the universe. The three characteristics of existence—*sattva* (goodness), *rajas* (passion), and *tamas* (ignorance)—are said to be embodied in Lord Vishnu. He is thought to permeate every living thing, from the tiniest atom to the huge cosmos. Maintaining the delicate balance between the forces of creation and destruction is crucial to his position as the universe's defender and preserver.

Vishnu belonged to the family of celestial gods known as the Adityas, which sprang from Aditi's womb and were twelve in number (all males). He is thought to have taken many different incarnations on earth, known as his avatars, in order to bring harmony and order to the cosmos.

Avatars of Lord Vishnu

According to Hindu mythology, Vishnu has assumed ten significant avatars collectively referred to as the Dashavatara to reestablish balance in the cosmos. Each avatar corresponds to a certain historical era and reflects a different facet of Vishnu's divinity. The ten avatars are Matsya (fish), Kurma (tortoise), Varaha (boar), Narasimha (half-lion, half-man), Vamana (dwarf), Parashurama (warrior sage), Rama (the hero of the *Ramayana*), Krishna (the hero of the *Mahabharata*), Balarama (Krishna's elder brother), and Kalki (the destroyer of evil). Buddha is occasionally added to the list of Lord Vishnu's avatars in place of Balarama due to the influence of certain sects that regard Buddha as an incarnation of Vishnu. However, Balarama is most commonly believed to be the ninth avatar of Vishnu.

Matsya: The Fish

In Hindu mythology, Matsya, which is Lord Vishnu's original avatar, is a key figure that is believed to have appeared in the *Satya Yuga* (3,747,102 BCE). The Sanskrit term *matsya* means "fish," and the avatar is shown as a huge fish with a human face. The Hindu creation myth, which sees the universe as being destroyed and recreated in a cyclical process, is the source of Matsya's tale.

Matsya is honored in festivals and rituals all over India, where he is revered as a representation of fertility and abundance.

An image of Matsya.
https://commons.wikimedia.org/wiki/File:Matsya_avatar.jpg

The Vedas, which are regarded as timeless truths, were conveyed orally for tens of thousands of years prior to Veda Vyasa's legendary compilation of them in writing. The Vedas were allegedly taken from the universe's creator, Brahma, by the demon Hayagriva. Lord Vishnu took the form of Matsya and dove into the ocean in search of the Vedas. Matsya informed King Manu of an impending flood and gave him the order to construct a boat that could accommodate various varieties of seeds, medicinal herbs, seven saints, the serpent Vasuki, and other animals. And so, Matsya became the protector of life, saving Manu and these other living things.

Water, which stands for both the power of creation and the source of life, is strongly related to Matsya. The fish is regarded as a representation of fertility and abundance. In Hindu art, Matsya is frequently seen holding a conch shell in one hand and a halo of water in the other, signifying his role as the guardian of life. The Matsya avatar has received a lot of praise in contemporary culture, notably in literature, film, and the visual arts.

Kurma: The Tortoise

The second of Lord Vishnu's ten avatars in Hindu mythology is Kurma, also known as Kurmavatara. This avatar also appears in the *Satya Yuga*. The Puranas tell the tale of Kurma, which is regarded as a significant incident in Hindu mythology.

The mythical tale of Samudra Manthan ("the churning of the ocean") serves as the basis for Kurma's origin. According to tradition, the Devas (gods) and the Asuras (demons) collaborated to churn the ocean and acquire the nectar of immortality. The mountain that was being utilized as the churning rod began to sink into the ocean. According to legend, Lord Vishnu transformed into a tortoise and supported the mountain on his back to prevent it from sinking.

An image of Kurma.
https://commons.wikimedia.org/wiki/File:Kurma_Avatar_by_Raja_Ravi_Varma.jpg

The tortoise symbolizes stability, steadfastness, and perseverance. It is viewed as a representation of Lord Vishnu's omnipotence and capacity to support the weight of the entire universe. The use of the tortoise also serves as a metaphor for the earth, which is shown to be perched on the back of a huge tortoise.

The concept of Kurma as an avatar has transformed and been reinterpreted over time in a variety of cultural and creative contexts. Various works of art, such as paintings, sculptures, and folk art, have portrayed the Kurma myth. Throughout India, the avatar can be seen in numerous temples and structures.

Additionally, the narrative of Kurma has been understood from a spiritual perspective in addition to its cultural relevance. The concept of selflessness (in this case, being prepared to carry the weight of the world for the greater good) is represented in the story. It also represents the path taken by the soul on its way to enlightenment.

Varaha: The Boar

In Hindu mythology, Varaha, often known as the Boar, is Lord Vishnu's third form. The word *Varaha* is a proto-Indo-Iranian term for boar (*warajha*). The Varaha avatar, which resembles a boar with a human body, is revered as the guardian of the earth. The concept of this avatar dates to the time of *Satya Yuga*.

One day, the earth was allegedly taken by the demon Hiranyaksha, who concealed it in the depths of the cosmic ocean. Lord Vishnu, assuming the shape of a boar, dove into the ocean to collect the earth. He engaged in a bloody conflict with the demon Hiranyaksha before ultimately defeating him and freeing the earth from his control.

This avatar of Lord Vishnu symbolizes strength and protection. It stands for Lord Vishnu's ability to save the universe from bad influences. The boar represents power, aggression, and tenacity.

Varaha was regarded as a strong and protective sign in antiquity. The earth was thought to be shielded from calamities like floods, earthquakes, and volcanic eruptions by Varaha. Many Hindus still worship Varaha in the modern era. Worshiping the Varaha avatar is thought to aid in overcoming challenges and achieving success in life.

Varaha has appeared in many different forms in contemporary Indian art and culture. The boar-headed Vishnu is shown in paintings, sculptures, and murals. He is shown in some artistic mediums as a ferocious warrior, while in others, he is portrayed as a kind protector. The story behind this avatar serves as a reminder of the need to defend the planet and the need to combat evil powers that pose a threat to the universe.

Narasimha: The Man-Lion

In Hindu mythology, Narasimha, also known as the Man-Lion, is the fourth form of Lord Vishnu's ten avatars and is believed to have appeared in the *Treta Yuga* (2,055,102 BCE). The English name "Narasimha" is formed by combining the Sanskrit words *nara*, meaning "man," and *simha*, meaning "lion." The Narasimha avatar is portrayed as having a human body and a lion's head and is revered as a defender of his followers.

In accordance with the Hindu legend, Hiranyakashipu, the demon king, desired to murder his own son, Prahlada, who was a follower of Lord Vishnu. Hiranyakashipu attained a blessing that made it impossible for him to be slain by anyone or anything at any time of day or night, inside or outside, or by any kind of weapon. At dusk, when it was neither night nor day, Lord Vishnu took the shape of Narasimha, an entity that was neither human nor animal, and killed Hiranyakashipu at the entrance of his palace.

The Narasimha avatar is the representation of protection and justice. It stands for Lord Vishnu's ability to defend his followers from evil powers and promote justice across the cosmos. The human body is a representation of intelligence, wisdom, and compassion, while the lion stands for power, bravery, and fearlessness.

Many Hindus still revere Narasimha in the modern era. Worshiping the Narasimha avatar is thought to foster courage and inner power. For Hindus, the tale of Narasimha serves as a reminder of the value of safeguarding believers and supporting the rule of law.

Vamana: The Dwarf Priest

Lord Vishnu's fifth incarnation in Hindu mythology is Vamana, who is often known as the Dwarf. It is commonly believed that the avatar appeared during the *Treta Yuga*. The Vamana avatar is seen as a representation of humility and selflessness, and it is thought that he took on a human form to impart to humans the value of these attributes.

Bali, the demon king, was said to have acquired invincibility and took over the universe. Vamana requested land he could traverse in three steps when in King Bali's court. Bali granted the request, thinking about what could possibly be covered in three steps. With his first and second steps, Vamana, who had become enormous, covered the earth and the void between it and the heavens. Bali volunteered his head as the third step because Vamana had nowhere else to go for the third step. Vamana put his foot on Bali's head and dispatched him to rule the underworld. In this incarnation, Vamana is referred to as Trivikrama, the "God of the Three Strides."

This avatar represents modesty and selflessness. It serves as a reminder of the value of living simply and giving without expecting anything in return. The Dwarf is a representation of how modest material aspirations are in relation to spiritual wealth's immeasurable riches.

Vamana has been portrayed in many different ways in contemporary Indian art and culture. He is portrayed in diverse stances in sculptures, paintings, and mosaics to represent his many different characteristics. He is shown in certain artistic mediums as a kind and serene divine figure, but in others, he is portrayed as a fearsome warrior.

A sculpture of what is believed to be Vamana.
Sudhamshu Hebbar, CC BY 2.0 <https://creativecommons.org/licenses/by/2.0>, via Wikimedia Commons; https://commons.wikimedia.org/wiki/File:Vamana_Avatar.jpg

Parashurama: Rama with an Ax

One of the ten avatars of Lord Vishnu is Parashurama, also known as Rama with the ax or the "Angry Man." The word "Parashurama" is a combination of the words *parashu*, which means "ax," and Rama, which refers to the protagonist of the epic *Ramayana*. Hindu mythology holds that Lord Vishnu took the form of Parashurama during the *Treta Yuga* when evil and corruption were rampant in the universe.

The tale of Parashurama's birth is told in various Hindu scriptures, but the *Mahabharata* is the most widely read version. This account claims that the sage Jamadagni and his wife Renuka were the parents of Parashurama. Jamadagni, a follower of Lord Shiva, gave Parashurama extensive instruction in martial arts, combat, and devotion. A troop of Kshatriyas (members of the warrior caste), led by King Kartavirya Arjuna, visited Jamadagni's ashram (a place where individuals withdraw spiritually or religiously) one day when Parashurama was gone and requested hospitality.

Jamadagni was a gracious sage, and he welcomed them and provided them with food. The divine cow Kamadhenu, which belonged to Jamadagni, was seen by the Kshatriyas, who desired it and took it by force. King Kartavirya was slain by Parashurama with his ax in a fit of fury. After learning that a Brahmin had killed a warrior, Sage Jamadagni ordered Parashurama on a journey to be purified. When he got back, Parashurama learned that his father had been murdered by Kartavirya's sons. Parashurama slaughtered every warrior from the king's tribe out of rage.

Parashurama's ax, which he handled with tremendous skill and savagery, serves as his emblem. His function as a hunter of evil and defender of good is represented by the ax. A common representation of Parashurama is a powerful man with matted hair, a lengthy beard, and a ferocious look. He is often pictured clutching an ax in one hand.

An image of Parashurama.
https://commons.wikimedia.org/wiki/File:Parashurama_with_axe.jpg

Lord Rama: The Perfect Man

Lord Rama, who is considered one of the most revered deities in Hinduism, is believed to be the seventh incarnation of Lord Vishnu and is also known as Ramachandra. He is frequently referred to as the "Perfect Man" because of his devotion to dharma (righteousness) and his wonderful personality. The avatar is believed to have appeared in the *Treta Yuga*.

Hindu mythology states that Lord Rama was born to King Dasharatha and Queen Kausalya in the northern Indian city of Ayodhya. He was the oldest of four brothers, and his guru (a spiritual teacher), Vishwamitra, instructed him in martial arts and spirituality. Lord Rama is renowned for his unmatched love of his parents, his wife Sita, his brother Lakshmana, and all of creation. In addition, he is well known for his legendary conflict with Ravana, the demon king who kidnapped Sita.

An image of Rama.
https://commons.wikimedia.org/wiki/File:Lord_Rama_with_arrows.jpg

Rama's bow and arrow, which he employed to wipe out evil forces and maintain dharma, serve as his emblem. He is usually seen alongside his wife Sita, his brother Lakshmana, and a fervent follower named Hanuman. Rama has a blue or dark complexion, signifying his ties to Vishnu.

Lord Rama's tale was frequently used as evidence of the significance of upholding one's obligations and adhering to dharma. He was connected to the *bhakti* (devotion or love) movement in medieval times, which emphasized the value of devotion over conventional practices. Lord Rama has come to represent Hindu nationalism in modern times, with his image being exploited to assert Hindu supremacy over other religions and to promote the Hindu identity.

Lord Krishna: The Divine Statesman

One of Hinduism's most beloved gods is Lord Krishna, who is thought to be Lord Vishnu's eighth avatar that appeared in the *Dvapara Yuga* (the third *yuga*). His heavenly nature, intelligence, and role as a leader and warrior are well known. The historical epic *Mahabharata*, as well as the *Bhagavata Purana* and other writings, recount the tale of Lord Krishna.

Hindu mythology states that in the northern Indian city of Mathura, King Vasudeva and Queen Devaki gave birth to Krishna. Father Vasudev escorted Lord Krishna across the turbulent River Yamuna to Gokul in a basket for his protection. Yashoda and Nanda adopted Krishna and brought him up in Gokul. Lord Krishna is renowned for his fondness of cowherd girls (*gopis*), his flute playing, and his fun and mischievous personality.

Lord Krishna's flute and peacock feather serve as symbols. He frequently appears with his beloved Radha, his brother Balarama, and Arjuna, one of his devoted followers. His blue skin suggests that he is connected to Lord Vishnu.

A statue of Krishna at the Sri Mariamman Temple in Singapore.
AngMoKio, CC BY-SA 3.0 <https://creativecommons.org/licenses/by-sa/3.0>, via Wikimedia Commons; https://commons.wikimedia.org/wiki/File:Sri_Mariamman_Temple_Singapore_2_amk.jpg

His teachings in the Bhagavad Gita (a script of seven hundred verses that is a part of the epic *Mahabharata*) were once regarded as a manual for kings and warriors.

The Bhagavad Gita contains an illustration of Lord Krishna's tenacity. The parijata (a kind of lotus flower grown on the heavenly planets) was at the center of a dispute between Krishna and Indra, the king of Heaven. One of Krishna's queens, Satyabhama, asked for the flower, but Indra turned her down. As a result, Krishna and the gods, including the Pandavas (five brothers), engaged in a fierce conflict. In the end, Krishna triumphed, took the parijata flower, and gave it to Satyabhama. He gave Narada Muni the order to tell everyone, including non-devotees, that no demigod could force him to break his word to his queen. Thus, by keeping his word to Satyabhama, Krishna proved his dedication.

Generations of Hindus have been motivated by Krishna's teachings to delve deeper into the nature of reality and the meaning of life. Lord Krishna is still adored and worshiped by Hindus today.

Balarama: Krishna's Elder Brother

Balarama, also known as Baladeva or Balabhadra, is an avatar of Lord Vishnu. He also appeared in the *Dvapara Yuga*. He is frequently shown as a tall, powerful man pulling a plow and is said to be Lord Krishna's older brother.

King Vasudeva and his wife Rohini gave birth to Balarama. He was nurtured in Gokul with his younger brother Krishna under the care of his foster mother, Yashoda. Balarama became renowned for his power and his prowess with a plow, which he used to cultivate the land and defend his people from harm. Balarama wields a plow as his weapon, employing it in various acts. According to the *Bhagavata Purana*, he utilized it to combat demons, create a path for the Yamuna River to reach Gokul, and even shift the entire capital of Hastinapura into the Ganges River.

Lord Vishnu took on the form of Balarama for several reasons. He wanted to get rid of Ravana, the demon king, and help King Yadu run his country. Both goals were accomplished by Lord Vishnu through the avatar of Balarama.

Balarama is seen as a representation of strength and defense. He is frequently linked to the sun, the moon, and the earth, as well as with agriculture. In certain stories, he is also linked to the serpent and is seen as having the ability to tame and control it.

Kalki: The Mighty Warrior

Kalki, also known as Kalkin, is regarded as the final and tenth incarnation of Lord Vishnu. He is thought to be a strong warrior who will make an appearance at the conclusion of the *Kali Yuga*, the current era of darkness and destruction, to bring order back to the universe.

Kalki is depicted as riding a white horse with a sword in his hand. He is portrayed as a savior who will arrive to defeat evil and usher in a brand-new era of stability and harmony.

An image of Kalki on his white horse.
https://commons.wikimedia.org/wiki/File:Kalki_Avatar_by_Ravi_Varma.jpg

Hindu mythology attributes the final victory of good over evil to Kalki, who is frequently portrayed as a figure of hope. He is also viewed as a divine figure who will bring back the universe's natural equilibrium and lead people toward a more peaceful and prosperous future.

Conclusion

The tales of Vishnu's avatars serve as a testament to Indian mythology's enduring beauty. They serve as an insight into the rich and colorful world of gods, goddesses, and heroes and remind us of the virtues of love, fidelity, and righteousness.

Lord Vishnu is worshiped by devotees through a variety of rites and offerings, including chanting his name, reciting his hymns, and giving him flowers and fruits.

Chapter 3: Shiva the Destroyer

Lord Shiva is one of the three principal deities of Hinduism, along with Brahma and Vishnu. He is considered the god of destruction and renewal and is often depicted as a yogi (a practitioner of yoga) who meditates on the peak of Mount Kailash. Many people consider Shiva to be the god of yoga and the arts.

Shiva can be recognized by a number of distinguishing features, including the third eye on his forehead, the snake Vasuki wrapped around his neck, the crescent moon gracing his brow, and the trident that he holds. He is typically venerated as an icon called a lingam. Shiva's teachings emphasize the importance of letting go of attachment and embracing change, both on a personal and universal level. Shiva represents truth, goodness, and beauty and is responsible for the destruction of the ego.

There are many festivals and rituals dedicated to Shiva throughout the year, with the most famous being Maha Shivaratri, or the Great Night of Shiva. This festival is celebrated in late winter and is a time for fasting, meditation, and prayer. To obtain Shiva's blessing and protection, worshipers offer him prayers, flowers, and delicacies.

Image of Shiva.
https://www.pexels.com/photo/photo-of-lord-shiva-statue-in-india-7104962/

Shiva: The Lord of Destruction

The Trimurti is the trinity of the three major gods in Hinduism: Brahma, Vishnu, and Shiva. Brahma is regarded as the creator of the universe, Vishnu as the preserver, and Shiva as the quintessential destroyer. When the end of time comes, Shiva's job is to dissolve all the worlds into nothingness. This idea is in line with current theories of space, which postulate that the expansion of a massive black hole that is consuming material from countless galaxies may cause the end of the physical universe within a few billion years. To Hindus, Shiva may be acting in that capacity as the black hole or as its creator.

It is easy to assume that Shiva's role is limited to destruction, but this is not the case. Shiva has several tasks to accomplish before the world truly comes to an end. His main duty is to eliminate everything to maintain Rta or the order of the universe. Shiva's destruction of things is a positive force that feeds and develops energy for the benefit of the world and its inhabitants. Shiva's devastation aids in nature's evolution, change, and transformation, as well as the smooth passage of objects and occurrences from one phase to the next.

Shiva destroys people's flaws so they can progress spiritually. He destroys their delusions, desires, and ignorance, as well as their evil and negative nature. Shiva also aids in people's personal development by purging their minds of old memories and detaching them from impurities, negative karma, emotions, and any other obstacles that hinder their growth. With his help, it is believed people can move forward and achieve inner enlightenment without any conflict. Shiva can even eliminate death itself. He is the source of life and existence and is thus associated with vitality.

Lord Shiva: The Ascetic Yogi

Lord Shiva is widely revered as an ascetic yogi and is considered the first yogi. It is claimed that Shiva became a traveling ascetic by giving up all worldly pleasures and material goods. He is often depicted as living in remote forests and mountains, meditating for extended periods of time, and subsisting on meager offerings from the natural world. His characteristic attire of a simple loincloth, matted hair, and ash-smeared body demonstrates his ascetic lifestyle.

One of the most significant events in Shiva's life is his meditation on Mount Kailash. Legend has it that Shiva meditated on the mountain for centuries, attaining a state of deep spiritual awareness and enlightenment. During this period, he was known as Adiyogi, or the first yogi, and is said to have imparted the knowledge of yoga to his first disciples, the Saptarishis or the seven sages.

Another important episode in Shiva's life is his encounter with Tripura, three cities that were constructed by Mayasura, a brilliant architect. These cities were prosperous but also impious. Shiva destroyed Tripura with his yogic powers, thereby restoring balance to the universe.

Shiva managed this feat when the gods told him that the Asuras had become evil and stopped worshiping the Vedas. They asked him to stop the Asuras, and Shiva agreed to do so. Shiva asked Vishvakarma, the architect of the gods, to make him a chariot, a bow, and arrows. Vishvakarma obliged, creating a chariot out of pure gold. With Brahma leading it, Shiva rode toward Tripura. At the exact second that the three cities aligned (the cities constantly moved around and only sat in a straight line for a few moments every one thousand years), Shiva launched the Pashupatastra, his most deadly arrow, into the three cities, destroying and burning them instantly.

Another tale suggests that as the cities merged, Lord Shiva only smiled, and his smile set the cities on fire, thus burning them and destroying Tripura.

The Many Forms of Lord Shiva

Lord Shiva is a complex and multifaceted deity with a rich mythology. He is revered by tens of millions of Hindus around the world and is considered an important symbol of the cyclical nature of existence.

Shiva as Mahadeva

Shiva, as Mahadeva, is a prominent deity in Hinduism and holds a significant place in the Shaivite sects of India. Lord Shiva is considered the embodiment of the Supreme Being (Brahma), representing the destructive element of the Trimurti. Mahadeva is associated with destruction, but this is not seen as a negative act but rather as a necessary step in the cycle of creation and renewal.

Some scholars believe that as Mahakala, he destroys and dissolves everything into nothingness, but as Shankara, he reproduces that which has been destroyed and dissolved. Therefore, he is both the creator and the destroyer of the universe.

The lingam, the phallus-shaped symbol of Shiva, represents his reproductive power, which is critical for the cycle of life and creation. As Mahadeva, he is the paramount lord who governs the forces of destruction and creation and the cycles of life and death. He is the ultimate source of all energy and power.

Shiva as Nataraja

Nataraja is the dancing form of Lord Shiva and is one of his most famous and widely recognized depictions. The word "Nataraja" is derived from the Sanskrit words *nata*, which means "dance," and *raja*, which means "king." This representation of Lord Shiva is one of the most well-known Hindu icons, and bronze sculptures of it are still made in some regions of southern India, particularly in the Chidambaram region.

A Chola sculpture of the dancing form of Lord Shiva.
https://en.wikipedia.org/wiki/File:Shiva_as_the_Lord_of_Dance_LACMA_edit.jpg

The Nataraja form of Lord Shiva is considered to be a masterpiece of Chola art. Chola was one of the most powerful Tamil kingdoms during medieval times, hailing from southern India. The Chola sculptures are renowned for their exquisite beauty and intricate detailing.

Shiva as Ardhanarishvara

Ardhanarishvara is a unique and fascinating representation of Lord Shiva and his consort Parvati, the goddess of power and fertility. This deity is often depicted as a figure that combines both masculine and feminine features. The term *Ardhanarishvara* literally means "half-man, half-woman" in Sanskrit.

The iconic image of Ardhanarishvara portrays the god with the right half of his body resembling Shiva, complete with his trademark matted hair, third eye, and trident, while the left half resembles Parvati, with her feminine curves and adorned with jewelry and flowers. This unique fusion symbolizes the inseparable nature of the masculine and feminine energies that exist within the universe, known as Purusha and Prakrti, respectively.

The concept of Ardhanarishvara emphasizes the idea that the divine male and female principles are interconnected and interdependent and that both are necessary for the creation, sustenance, and transformation of the world. Ardhanarishvara is often associated with the idea of balance and harmony and the transcendence of duality, as, in this form, Shiva is half-woman and half-man, being both and neither at the same time. This deity is also sometimes revered as a symbol of divine unity and androgyny, as well as a powerful force for transformation and spiritual growth.

Shiva as Bhairava

Bhairava is a fierce form of Lord Shiva and is associated with death and destruction. He is commonly portrayed with a dog as his mount. Despite his terrifying appearance, Bhairava is renowned as the protector of women and children, and his worship is believed to offer them security and safety. The term *bhairava* is a Sanskrit word meaning "terrible" or "frightful."

According to Hindu mythology, Bhairava was created by Lord Shiva to guard the holy city of Varanasi (also known as Kashi) from negative energies and malevolent spirits. The city is considered to be a sacred site for Hindus, and Bhairava's presence is believed to sanctify and safeguard it. Bhairava is thought to be the protector of the eight cardinal directions, which include north, south, east, west, northeast, northwest, southeast, and southwest. As the guardian of directions, Bhairava is regarded as an omnipresent and all-seeing deity who protects devotees from harm and negative influences.

Despite Bhairava's fearsome reputation, he is revered for his benevolence and compassion. He is often worshiped as a deity who can bestow blessings and boons upon devotees who seek his aid.

Shiva as Pashupati

The term Pashupati is derived from the Sanskrit words *pashu*, meaning "animal," and *pati*, meaning "lord" or "master." Thus, Pashupati is often referred to as the "lord of the animals," reflecting Lord Shiva's close association with the natural world.

Lord Shiva's affiliation with the bull known as Nandi, who is frequently shown as his mount, is one of the most notable ways in which he is connected to animals. The bull symbolizes strength, virility, and fertility and is considered a sacred animal in Hinduism. The bull also represents the steadfast devotion of Lord Shiva's devotees, who are believed to be like Nandi in their loyalty and dedication.

Lord Shiva is also associated with the tiger, which represents power, strength, and fierceness. Tigers are seen as powerful predators in nature and are often used to represent Lord Shiva's fierce and unyielding nature, as well as his role as the protector of the universe.

How Shiva Turned Blue

According to tradition, the Devas and the Asuras, who were cousins, were in constant conflict. However, they eventually agreed to work together to churn the ocean of milk and extract Amrit, the nectar of immortality. They believed that whoever drank it would become immortal and all-powerful. However, Amrit could only be obtained by churning the ocean of milk.

To begin the process, the Devas and the Asuras decided to use Mount Mandara as a churning rod. Lord Vishnu, one of the most important Hindu deities, took the form of a giant tortoise to support the mountain and prevent it from sinking. The serpent king Vasuki, who had a thousand heads, offered himself as the rope to rotate the churning rod. The Devas and the Asuras began vigorously churning the ocean of milk while holding onto Vasuki's head and tail.

As they churned the ocean, a great many things emerged, including precious gems, rare animals, and even the goddess of wealth, Lakshmi. However, the Devas and the Asuras were not satisfied with these treasures; they desired only Amrit. Suddenly, to their horror, the ocean of milk began to churn up a deadly poison called Halahala. The poison was so powerful that it could destroy the entire world. The Devas and Asuras were engulfed in the poisonous cloud, and they began to choke and suffer.

At that moment, Lord Shiva appeared. When he saw the Devas and Asuras in agony, he knew he had to act quickly to save the world. He drank the poison that had emerged from the ocean of milk to prevent it from spreading further. However, the poison was so potent that it began to burn Shiva's insides. He realized that he needed to get rid of the poison before it caused any more damage.

Shiva's consort, Parvati, quickly realized what was happening and clasped her hand around Shiva's neck to prevent the poison from going down his throat. The poison could not pass beyond Parvati's grasp, and as a result, Shiva's throat turned blue, and he earned the name Neela-kanta, which means "blue neck" or "blue throat."

Lord Shiva's sacrifice saved the world from destruction, and he gained a permanent reminder of his selfless act in the form of his blue throat. The story of Lord Shiva and the churning of the ocean of milk is an essential part of Hindu mythology.

Marriage of Shiva and Parvati

The marriage of Shiva and Parvati is one of the most popular stories in Hindu mythology. It is said that Parvati, the daughter of the mountain king Himalaya, was smitten by the handsome and powerful Shiva at a very young age. However, Shiva was a hermit who lived in the mountains and was known for his detachment from worldly affairs. He had no interest in marriage or relationships.

Despite Shiva's lack of interest, Parvati was determined to win his heart. She performed intense penance and devotion to Shiva for years, hoping to impress him. She underwent great physical and mental hardships, and her devotion to Shiva was so intense that she even abandoned her luxurious lifestyle and lived like an ascetic.

However, despite all her efforts, Shiva remained unmoved. He saw no need for a companion in his life. Parvati was undeterred and continued to pursue Shiva relentlessly, and her devotion grew stronger with each passing day.

Finally, after years of penance and devotion, Parvati's determination and love for Shiva moved him. He appeared before her and agreed to marry her. Their union is said to have symbolized the union of the male and female principles of creation, which is an essential aspect of Hindu mythology.

Maha Shivratri, one of the most significant holidays in Hinduism, commemorates the union of Shiva and Parvati each year. It is believed that Shiva and Parvati were married on this day, and it is a day of great spiritual significance for devotees of Lord Shiva.

The union of Shiva and Parvati is also important because it resulted in the birth of their two sons, Ganesha and Kartikeya, and their daughter, Ashokasundari. Ganesha is one of the most popular gods in Hinduism and is worshiped as the god of wisdom and success, while Kartikeya is worshiped as the god of war.

Lord Shiva and the Snakes

Snakes have always been considered sacred in Indian culture. Lord Shiva is often depicted with snakes coiled around his neck. This imagery has a significant symbolic meaning and is associated with several stories and legends.

Samudra Manthan, the churning of the ocean, is one of the most well-known legends that explains why Shiva has snakes around his neck. In this tale, the gods and demons were vying for the ocean's nectar of immortality. Several priceless items, including a deadly poison that could wipe out the universe, emerged from the ocean during the churning. Shiva, the universe's guardian, ingested the poison to safeguard the universe.

As the poison was spreading through his body, Vasuki, the king of the snakes, came forward and offered to help him. Vasuki coiled around Shiva's neck and prevented the poison from spreading to his head. This act impressed Shiva, and he blessed and accepted the snake as his adornment.

It is also said that Shiva made ornaments out of the poisonous snake and presented them to his wife Parvati as a gift. The snake on his neck, therefore, represents Shiva's love for his wife.

Vasuki around Shiva's neck.
Foliate08, CC BY-SA 3.0 <https://creativecommons.org/licenses/by-sa/3.0>, via Wikimedia Commons; https://commons.wikimedia.org/wiki/File:Shiva_01.JPG

Covered in Ash

Lord Shiva is often depicted as being covered in ash, which is symbolic of his renunciation of material possessions and his ascetic lifestyle. This depiction of Lord Shiva has its origin in a Hindu story that illustrates the importance of humility and the dangers of pride.

According to tradition, a powerful sage named Parnada was cutting grass when he accidentally cut his finger. Instead of blood, the sap of a tree oozed out. This incident filled Parnada with pride, and he believed that he had become the most pious man in the world, as he did not bleed as people do. Lord Shiva, who witnessed this incident, decided to teach the sage a lesson.

Lord Shiva took the disguise of an old man and asked the sage about the reason for his delight. The sage replied that he had become the most pious man in the world because he no longer bled like a normal human. The old man questioned the sage's joy, saying that it was just sap and nothing to be proud of. He then demonstrated this by slicing his own finger and spilling ash instead of blood.

The sage realized his mistake and begged the god for forgiveness. Lord Shiva forgave the sage and covered him in ash to remind him of the importance of humility and the dangers of pride. The ash also symbolizes the transient nature of material possessions and the ultimate reality of death.

Nataraja and Tandava

Nataraja is one of the most popular representations of Shiva. In this form, Shiva is depicted as a graceful dancer surrounded by a fiery ring that represents the cycle of birth, death, and rebirth. This ring of flames is said to be a metaphor for the eternal energy that permeates the universe.

Nataraja's dance is not just a symbol of beauty and grace but also represents the dynamic interplay between the forces of creation and destruction. Through his dance, he creates new life, sustains it, and ultimately destroys it to make way for a new beginning. In this sense, Nataraja is seen as the embodiment of the eternal process of creation and destruction, which is central to Hindu philosophy.

The tiny demon Apasmara Purusha, which Nataraja is depicted standing upon, represents the negative qualities of ignorance, laziness, and evil thoughts. By dancing on the demon, Nataraja symbolizes his triumph over these negative qualities and his power to overcome them.

The dance of Lord Shiva, known as the Tandava, is said to represent the cosmic dance of creation, preservation, and destruction. The Tandava is a fierce and energetic dance that represents the destruction of the universe. Contrarily, Parvati performs the Lasya, which is a graceful and gentle dance that represents the beauty and joy of creation.

If Lord Shiva were to stop dancing, it is believed the universe would come to an end. Without his constant movement, the world would become stagnant and lifeless, and chaos would reign supreme. Therefore, it is said that Lord Shiva's dance is essential for the survival of the universe and that it will continue for eternity.

Conclusion

Shiva is known for his asceticism, his profound knowledge of yoga and meditation, and his compassion toward his devotees. His stories teach us about the importance of overcoming our ego and desires and embracing our true nature.

Shiva is also revered as the lord of dance and music, and his cultural significance goes beyond his role in Hindu mythology. Numerous pieces of music, literature, and art have been influenced by him, and he has had an impact on many different aspects of Indian culture.

Chapter 4: Hindu Goddesses
Part I

Goddesses in Hindu mythology play a vital role in the maintenance of the world and contribute to various aspects of life and living. They are not lesser in power or stature to male deities. Goddesses often hold power over matters of nurturance, procreation, fertility, wealth, and knowledge.

However, not all goddesses mean well. Goddesses can bring happiness and prosperity, but they are also capable of creating great chaos and unrest. Additionally, many of these goddesses appear under various names and titles and as various avatars.

Durga

The goddess Durga.
https://en.wikipedia.org/wiki/File:Durga_Mahisasuramardini.JPG

The goddess Durga goes by many names in the Hindu tradition. The more famous ones include Devi and Shakti, which together mean divine power. Her role in Indian mythology is acting as a commanding force of good, and her existence signifies purity in a world of chaos and destruction. Durga was created as an energy form and unconquerable force of the Supreme Being, Brahma, to supplement the creation and maintenance of the world.

Durga is often referred to as a protective mother. She is the protector of all that is good, pure, and harmonious. The Puranas offer various stories of the creation of Durga, though each of these portrays her as being created as a protector.

One story suggests Durga was created from Shiva's left half of his body. He later created Shiva Loka, at Mount Kailash, with Durga. In another story, the demonic chaos created by Mahishasura, a demon who used his deceit and cunning to defeat the gods, forced Vishnu to take action. He emitted a powerful light from his mouth, whose rays merged and morphed into the goddess Durga, who was able to challenge Mahishasura to a fight. She defeated his vast armies and cut off his head, thus ending his tyranny.

Etymology

The name Durga itself bears witness to the power of the goddess, as it means invincible and indomitable. Deriving from the word *durg*, which means impassable or implies an unconquerable fortress, and the word *gam*, meaning to pass, the name Durga comes to mean one who is beyond defeat, which is the way the goddess is depicted in stories.

The name Durga appears in earlier Indian texts, such as the Vedas, but is not accompanied by her tales of heroism and power that are found in the Puranas. Vedic narrations of the goddess's role portray her as the supreme deity. In other occurrences, Durga is used to refer to different cosmic beings and entities, though they are all powerful and good.

Appearance

Durga is always portrayed with multiple limbs, which signifies her ability to tackle multiple threats at once. She is always prepared to protect the world from evil. Durga's number of arms ranges anywhere from eight to eighteen, and they hold a variety of weapons and divine objects, such as a bow and arrow, javelin, sword, shield, chakra, conch, and a noose. These items help her fight and defeat evil.

She is also portrayed with three eyes. The left eye shows desire by depicting a moon, the right stands for action with the sun, and the middle eye represents fire, which symbolizes knowledge. To show the might of her power, Durga also often appears riding upon a tiger or lion.

The Weapons of Durga

Each of Durga's weapons is meant to aid her against evil, but they also hold symbolic meaning. The conch, for example, represents her connection to the Supreme Being. She holds on to him in the form of sound, as the conch indicates Pranava, or cosmic sound. Durga does not hold the bow and arrow the way one typically would; both are held in one hand, which symbolizes Durga's control over the potential and kinetic aspects of energy.

The chakra or the discus found spinning on her finger symbolizes the world, and the way in which it is held shows her complete control and command over the world. With this control, Durga is able to keep evil at bay and allow the world to walk the path of righteousness. The sword depicts her knowledge, which is sharp and free of doubt, and the lotus shows that her success in defeating evil is certain and also constant, for evil cannot be controlled except by constant struggle.

Durga has also been shown to carry a thunderbolt, which is a sign of her conviction. The trident shows the three qualities of *tamas, rajas,* and *sattva* (inactivity, activity, and non-activity, when a state of harmony has been achieved, respectively) to heal and maintain the physical, mental, and spiritual aspects of life.

Avatars of Durga

Durga, like other gods and goddesses in Indian mythology, appears in many different forms or avatars. These relate to the reincarnation process, with Durga appearing in nine different forms. These *Navadurgas,* the collective name for Durga's nine manifestations, include the following:

- Skandamata (stage of motherhood)
- Kusumanda (as the *Mahashakti*)
- Shailaputri (her stage of childhood)
- Kalaratri (stage of destruction)
- Brahmacharini (her period of asceticism)
- Maha Gauri (stage of recovery)
- Katyayani (period as a warrior)

- Chandraghanta (as Shakti)
- Siddhidatri (stage of becoming Mahashakti)

Each of these nine forms is celebrated and worshiped in Hindu festivals, and each represents Durga's powers as a goddess.

Celebration of Durga

Many Hindu festivals celebrate Durga. Durga Puja is a four-day festival that occurs in September or October. The nine-day-long festival of Navratri is celebrated in remembrance of Durga's victory over Mahishasura, and each day celebrates each of her nine incarnations, which are each signified by a specific color.

Durga holds great significance in Hindu mythology and in the hearts of those who practice Hinduism.

Saraswati

Saraswati.
Jean-Pierre Dalbéra, CC BY 2.0 <https://creativecommons.org/licenses/by/2.0>, via Wikimedia Commons; https://commons.wikimedia.org/wiki/File:2_Hindu_deity_Sarasvati_Saraswati_on_ceramic_tile_in_Munnar_Kerala_India_March_2014.jpg

The goddess Saraswati embodies wisdom and is also the goddess of music, speech, and learning. She is often referred to by other names and titles, including Bharati and Shatarupa, which can together mean eloquent existence. Saraswati is also often known as the mother of the Vedas. The Rig Veda contains the first and earliest known mention of the goddess. Later texts credit her with other attributes and achievements as well, such as the invention of Sanskrit. As the goddess of speech, language and learning are her domains, and she is believed to have gifted pen and ink to one of Shiva's children, Ganesha.

While many traditions believe her to be the wife of Brahma, other traditions, such as the Vaishnavas, believe her to have been the wife of Vishnu first. The wisdom shown by Saraswati is the embodiment of Durga's wisdom, and she represents only all that is good. Saraswati often appears in simple white garments, unadorned by jewelry or color, and moves beyond the materialistic world of desire.

The Creation of Saraswati

Saraswati came into being in response to the chaos of the universe. Brahma sought to bring order into the world and was counseled by Durga to bring knowledge into it. From Brahma's mouth emerged Saraswati, riding a swan and dressed all in white, holding books in one hand to represent her wisdom and a veena (a string instrument) in the other to show her mastery of music. Under her guidance, Brahma learned the value of wisdom and began to think, sense, understand, and communicate, which allowed him to create order out of the chaos of the universe.

The melody that Saraswati produced created vital energy, *prana*, throughout the universe, allowing the world to take shape. Since Saraswati was the first being to enter Brahma's world, he became enamored with her and began to desire her. Saraswati rejected his advances, and she did not give in to material desires. She attempted to hide from Brahma as a cow. He followed her as a bull. When she turned into a mare, Brahma morphed into a horse. Despite the continuous chase, Brahma could not catch her in any of her many forms, and thus, she came to be known as Shatarupa, meaning one that can take many forms.

Saraswati and Brahma

Traditions regarding the nature of Saraswati and Brahma's relationship vary. While some portray her as trying to escape Brahma's lust, others show her as the wife of Vishnu. Since Vishnu already had two wives, he gave Saraswati to Brahma. The union of the two is believed to have produced Manu, from whom all of human civilization was born. Manu survived the famine that killed all of the humans through the nourishment of his mother, allowing him to continue his lineage.

Brahma is believed not to be worshiped as much as the other gods of the Trimurti. A curse is thought to have been placed on him by Saraswati. As the legend goes, Brahma is said to have turned to the gods when Saraswati failed to turn up on time for an important ritual. The delay of this ritual was unacceptable in his eyes. The gods gave him a new wife, Gayatri, to begin the ritual, but when Saraswati saw Brahma with another woman, she cursed him, saying that humanity should never worship him.

Avatars of Saraswati

Saraswati took on many forms. In her original form, she appears with grace and simplicity, dressed in white and riding upon a swan. In addition to the veena and books, she also appears with a rosary and water pot. Her many avatars include the following:

- Medha
- Savitri
- Brahmani
- Gayatri
- Maha Saraswati
- Vāc
- Para Saraswati
- Shatarupa
- Sharada
- Vani
- Aditi
- Bharati

Tales of Saraswati

There are many tales of Saraswati in which she saves the world from destruction. In one such story, Saraswati is able to save Brahma and the world from a demon. The demon intended to seek power so that he could conquer the three worlds—earth, heaven, and hell—and so attempted to appease Brahma to gain power. When the gods turned to Saraswati for help, she outwitted the demon by sitting on his tongue.

When Brahma turned to grant the demon's wish, all he was able to wish for was to never stay awake. The demon found it quite hard to speak with Saraswati sitting on his tongue! Brahma granted his wish, and the demon was put to eternal sleep. His plans to take over the world ended.

Saraswati is also known to have saved the world from annihilation by Shiva. The god found the world in a state of chaos. The people were filled with corruption, and Shiva believed there was nothing left to salvage. As a result, he decided to start over, beginning with the destruction of the existing world so that a new one could be created. He opened his third eye to unleash a fire that would destroy the world and everything living on it.

Saraswati took the form of a river of purity, as fires could only destroy the impure and corrupt. The fire was trapped under the waters and would remain so as long as the world remained peaceful and humans uncorrupted. However, Saraswati warned that should wisdom leave the world, it would be replaced with strife, corruption, and destruction.

Parvati

Parvati and her son, Ganesha.
https://commons.wikimedia.org/wiki/File:Goddess_Parvati_and_her_son_Ganesha.jpg

Parvati is the goddess of love, fertility, and determination. She is also the wife of Shiva and the mother of Kartikeya (also known as Skanda) and Ganesha, the god of war and the remover of obstacles, as well as Ashokasundari, the goddess of harmony. Parvati's name is believed to have been taken from *Parvata*, meaning "mountain." Parvati is also seen as a manifestation of Durga, but this is usually when Parvati is not the consort of Shiva. As the feminine half of Shiva, the two present the duality of existence, the masculine and the feminine.

Parvati is linked to both Durga and Kali, the goddess of time and death. In many depictions, she is seen alongside Shiva, with the two in an intimate embrace. Some depictions portray the two in greater intimacy, with one-half of the body bearing the male traits of Shiva and the other half those of Parvati. This portrayal of the two of them shows the inseparable and dependent nature of the two—neither can exist without the other. When Parvati appears with Shiva, she is seen with two arms, but when she is depicted alone, she can be seen with four arms, carrying various objects in each hand.

The Creation of Parvati

Parvati came into existence to be a wife to Shiva. Shiva withdrew from the world after the death of his first wife. He became lost in mourning and meditation, neglecting to keep an eye on the world, which, in his absence, was overrun by demons from the underworld. The demons created chaos and destruction and sought to take over the world.

In this tale, the gods turned to Shakti (a mother goddess) for help, who proclaimed that only a son of Shiva could defeat the demons and restore order to the universe. As a result, she morphed into Parvati and brought Shiva out of his seclusion to become his wife.

Shiva did not initially take to Parvati, even though she visited him every day in his cave, bringing him fruit. As frustration took over and the world delved deeper into destruction, Parvati asked Kama, the god of desire, for help. He shot an arrow of desire into Shiva, hoping to make him fall for Parvati. However, Shiva did not take kindly to this, and he destroyed Kama with his third eye.

Parvati removed herself from the world, retreating into a forest to sink into meditation and spirituality. She sought no nourishment or shelter. Her devotion finally moved Shiva, who took her as his wife. Together, they had Ganesha and Kartikeya, who defeated the demons of the underworld with the help of Kali.

Parvati and Ganesha

Many texts relate different versions of how Parvati and Shiva's first son, Ganesha, came to be. Some texts, likely written between 1100 and 1400 CE, suggest that Shiva was against having children and told Parvati to create a cloth doll to quench her desire. In this story, the doll becomes enchanted by Parvati's tears, as she longs for a real baby, and these tears transform the doll into her son, Ganesha. Parvati places Ganesha at the mouth of her cave as a guard, instructing him not to let in any strangers.

When Shiva comes to visit Parvati, he does not recognize his son, having never met him before. Ganesha does not recognize his father and refuses him entry. Angered at the commands of a stranger who will not let him see his wife, Shiva cuts off Ganesha's head. Parvati is devastated, so much so that Shiva promises he will make Ganesha whole. He finds the head of an elephant, which he uses to replace Ganesha's head. Thus, Ganesha is reborn and is referred to as the remover of obstacles, owing to the way in which his rebirth occurred.

Lakshmi

Lakshmi.

VedSutra, CC BY-SA 4.0 <https://creativecommons.org/licenses/by-sa/4.0>, via Wikimedia Commons; https://commons.wikimedia.org/wiki/File:Goddess_Lakshmi_is_the_Hindu_Goddess_of_Wealth_and_Prosperity_with_an_Owl_as_her_animal_ride_or_vahana.jpg

Lakshmi is heralded as the goddess of wealth and fortune. As the wife of Vishnu, she showed total devotion to him by taking on various forms to be with him in his many incarnations. For example, in Vishnu's dwarf form, Lakshmi appears from a lotus and is known as Padma or Kamala. In Hindu mythology, the lotus flower represents success and spirituality. The lotus also refers to fertility, representing all of creation in the world, which Vishnu helped create. When Vishnu appeared as the warrior Parashurama, she became his wife as Dharani.

Lakshmi also forms part of the Tridevi, along with Saraswati and Parvati, as the trinity of goddesses in Hindu mythology (the counterpart to the Trimurti). Lakshmi is also referred to in many instances as Lokamata, the mother of the world, and as Lola, which means fickle. The name refers to the ways in which she offers good fortune to people, which can be administered haphazardly.

Appearance

Lakshmi often appears with four arms and hands, much like other gods and goddesses in Hindu mythology. She carries a lotus in two of these hands, which symbolizes purity and success. Each of her four arms is symbolic, as they represent the four goals that every Hindu should follow and strive to achieve. These are dharma, or good conduct; *kama*, desire in life; *artha*, being successful through legitimate means; and *moksha*, which is the liberation from the cycle of life and death.

Unlike the other goddesses of the Tridevi, Lakshmi does not focus on the spiritual. Rather, her role is in the pursuit and achievement of more materialistic aspects. While she plays a maternal role, she is also focused on fulfillment and the granting of desires.

Creation and Rebirth of Lakshmi

The story of Lakshmi's birth and creation varies based on the different texts, most of which date between 300 BCE and 300 CE. In the *Mahabharata*, she comes from the stirring of the milky ocean by the gods.

Indra and Lakshmi were married and had long protected the world from demons. Indra was given sacred flowers by a sage as a gift. Displeased, he threw away the gift. This act of arrogance made the sage angry, who cast a curse on Indra, causing the flowers of the world to wither. This hurt Lakshmi, as one of her many forms included the garland, and she blamed Indra for the disrespect he had caused her. His arrogance made Lakshmi retreat into the milky ocean. Without her, the world was overrun by demons. The gods turned to Vishnu for help, who counseled them to stir the ocean, from which Lakshmi emerged. She rose from the foaming butter, clothed in white and radiating beauty. Vishnu took her under his protection. She resided on his chest, giving him the name Shrinivas, the resting place of Shri, one of the avatars of Lakshmi.

Chapter 5: Hindu Goddesses Part II

Hinduism's practice of goddess worship dates back to the Indus Valley civilization, which arose in the northwest of the Indian subcontinent in approximately 3300 BCE. Figurines of goddesses made of terracotta were discovered during archaeological digs at Indus Valley sites. It is believed they were used in religious rituals.

In the Vedic era, which started around 1500 BCE, the Hindu goddesses were still worshiped. A number of gods and goddesses are honored in hymns found in the Vedas. These hymns portray the goddesses as strong, imaginative, and nurturing deities who bestow favors on their followers.

The worship of goddesses evolved and formalized during the medieval era. Tantra, a spiritual practice that first appeared in India about the 5th century CE, played a part in this too. This is still practiced in Hindu ceremonies today. Harnessing the force of Shakti and achieving spiritual enlightenment are the goals of tantric practices, which include mantras, rituals, and meditations. By the medieval era, the worship of goddesses evolved into a central component of tantric practices, with each goddess representing a distinct facet of Shakti.

Hindus believe in many goddesses, most of whom are linked to motherhood, fertility, and love. Thus, the worship of goddesses is frequently linked to the achievement of worldly goals like money, success, good fortune, and happiness.

Shakti

Hinduism reveres Shakti, also known as Devi or Adi Parashakti, as the most important goddess and the embodiment of feminine strength and creativity. The myths and legends surrounding her have an intricate connection with the history of Hindu goddesses.

The Goddess Shakti.
Soumik Barua, CC BY-SA 4.0 <https://creativecommons.org/licenses/by-sa/4.0>, via Wikimedia Commons; https://commons.wikimedia.org/wiki/File:Adi_Shakti_the_Supreme_Spirit_without_attributes.jpg

Origin and Meaning

The Vedic period is when the idea of Shakti first emerged, personified as the cosmic energy that powers all creation. The goddess is revered as the supreme entity in the Hindu denomination known as Shaktism. Shaktism's origins can be found in the illustrious Indus Valley civilization, whose people placed a strong emphasis on the veneration of the mother goddess. But it wasn't until the medieval era that Shaktism began to emerge as a distinct Hindu tradition.

Many scriptures were written during the medieval period. The Tantras were a collection of ritual manuals that were written from as early as the 7th century CE until the 19th century. During the 18th and 19th centuries, several Shakti-Tantric texts were written with the aim of introducing tantric concepts to the public and increasing their popularity. That's how Shaktism began to grow.

The Bhakti movement, which placed a strong emphasis on devotion to a personal god or goddess, also contributed to the expansion of Shaktism. Devotional poems and hymns to the goddess were written by numerous poets and saints, which contributed to the spread of her admiration.

The Sanskrit word *shak*, which means "to be able" or "power," is where the name "Shakti" originates. Hindus believe that the fundamental, divine energy known as Shakti has the ability to create, maintain, and end the universe. She is linked to fertility, wealth, and the defense of the vulnerable and oppressed.

Attributes and Symbolism

Hindu mythology represents Shakti in several different ways, each with its own characteristics and symbolism. The most well-known manifestations of Shakti are Durga, Kali, Parvati, and Lakshmi.

The yantra and the mandala are two symbolic representations of the concept of Shakti. The mandala is a circular shape that symbolizes the world and how everything is interrelated, whereas the yantra is a geometric design that represents the energy field of Shakti.

Hindu mythology holds that Shakti was created through the fusion of the powers of Brahma, Vishnu, and Shiva.

Kali

The goddess Kali is considered a sacred and fierce goddess in Hinduism. She is frequently depicted as a furious and strong deity who represents both creation and destruction. Typical representations of Kali include her having several arms, wearing a necklace made of severed heads, and standing on a corpse or a demon.

The goddess Kali.
https://commons.wikimedia.org/wiki/File:Kali_by_Raja_Ravi_Varma.jpg

Origin and Meaning

Kali's origins can be found in early Hindu mythology, where it is thought that she is an incarnation of the goddess Durga. In the tale, the demon Mahishasura was so strong that he threatened to rule the universe. The Devas, commanded by Indra, were defeated by Mahishasura in the battle between the gods (Devas) and the demons (Asuras). The Devas combined their divine forces in an effort to find a solution, giving birth to the goddess Durga. Mahishasura was fought by Durga, and Durga prevailed, killing Mahishasura. After the struggle, Durga allegedly transformed into Kali due to her extreme fury.

The Sanskrit word *kala*, which means "time," is the source of Kali's name. The name of this goddess seems fitting because Kali is frequently linked to the universe's constant cycle of creation and destruction. Because of the transient nature of human existence, Kali is frequently portrayed with a necklace of skulls around her neck. Her dark skin serves as a further allegory for the night before morning.

Between about the 6th and 16th centuries CE, India saw the growth of Kali as a deity. Various Hindu literature and religious practices that emphasized the authority and significance of female deities, like Kali, came into being during this time. The *Devi Mahatmya*, which details the struggles of the goddess Durga against many demons and her transformation into Kali, is one important piece of literature from this era.

The story of Kali's conflict with the demon Raktabija is one of the most well-known mythical tales related to her. Raktabija had the ability to turn every drop of his blood that touched the earth into a new demon. Because of this, he was nearly impossible to beat. Raktabija was defeated when Kali drank all of his blood before it could hit the ground.

The concept of Kali has changed over time. In certain cultures, Kali is revered as a protective mother goddess who shields her followers from harm and drives away evil spirits. Other cultures see Kali as a destroyer goddess who brings about the end of the world to make space for a fresh cycle of creation.

With a complex mythology and a variety of manifestations, Kali is still regarded as a significant and widely venerated goddess in Hinduism today. Her roots are difficult to pinpoint in terms of certain historical periods, but her continued significance in Hinduism is a testament to the importance and strength of female deities.

Kamadhenu

Kamadhenu is referred to as the mother of cows or the wish-granting cow. In Hindu mythology, she is worshiped as a celestial entity who can grant the wishes of her followers.

Kamadhenu.

Kamdhenu, CC BY-SA 3.0 <https://creativecommons.org/licenses/by-sa/3.0>, via Wikimedia Commons; https://commons.wikimedia.org/wiki/File:Kamdhenu.jpg

The *Mahabharata*, a Hindu epic, is where Kamadhenu first appears. The gods churned the cosmic ocean while creating Kamadhenu. She was a gift presented to the sage Vasishta and became a representation of prosperity, fertility, and abundance. The goddess Lakshmi, who is connected to wealth and prosperity in Hindu mythology, is frequently associated with Kamadhenu.

Meaning and Depiction

The classic representation of Kamadhenu is a cow with four or more horns and a golden body. She is frequently depicted standing on a lotus or a throne, and she is occasionally joined by a calf or multiple cows. The terms *kama*, which means "desire," and *dhenu*, which means "cow," are the roots of the name "Kamadhenu." This name honors her capacity to grant the wishes of her followers.

Attributes and Symbolism

Her part in the tale of the sage Jamadagni and his son, Parashurama, is one of the most well-known stories connected to Kamadhenu. The milk of Kamadhenu, who belonged to Jamadagni, was thought to have extraordinary healing abilities. When Kamadhenu was taken from

Jamadagni's ashram one day, a group of soldiers known as the Kshatriyas drank her milk to treat their wounds. Angered by the robbery, Parashurama launched a campaign against the Kshatriyas, killing them all in the process.

The concept of Kamadhenu in Indian culture has changed over time. According to some beliefs, the goddess Durga is connected with Kamadhenu, who is viewed as a representation of maternity and care. Kamadhenu is revered during festivals and auspicious occasions as a source of material and spiritual wealth.

Kamadhenu continues to be highly regarded and honored in modern Indian culture. In India and other countries in southern Asia, her image can be found in many temples, shrines, and homes. Due to her connection to cows and the significance of cow worship in Hinduism, Kamadhenu has become a political lightning rod in India, with some groups fighting for the protection of cows and others opposing what they regard as the politicization of religious beliefs.

Sita

One of the most cherished goddesses in Hinduism is Sita. She is known as the spouse of Lord Rama, one of Lord Vishnu's incarnations. Her life, her love for her husband, and her devotion to dharma (righteousness) are all reasons why she is one of the most beloved goddesses in Hinduism.

Sita is renowned for her elegance, wisdom, bravery, and constancy. Her tales have been told and commemorated in numerous works of literature and art throughout the ages, and both Hindus and non-Hindus continue to be inspired by her. Millions of Hindus around the world hold Sita in the highest respect and consider her to be one of the most prominent goddesses in Hindu mythology.

Origin and Meaning

Although the precise dates and details are unknown, it is possible to trace the origins of Sita and the *Ramayana* back to ancient Indians. The *Ramayana* is thought to have been composed sometime between 400 and 200 BCE; however, other historians believe it may have been written as recently as the 4th century CE. Sita's story has been altered and reinterpreted by various communities and civilizations throughout India and Southeast Asia for millennia prior to it being written down.

Hindu mythology states that Sita was the daughter of King Janaka of Mithila, a nation that is now Nepal. She was regarded as a wonderful gift from the soil, as Janaka found her in a field that had been plowed. Lord Rama, the prince of Ayodhya, was drawn to Sita when she was a young woman and fell in love with her at first sight. Rama and Sita were wed in a lavish ceremony, but their joy did not last long. Sita made the decision to go into the jungle with Rama when he was banished from his country for fourteen years.

Sita was kidnapped by the demon king Ravana when they were in exile. When he first saw Sita in the forest, Ravana, the demon king with many heads and arms, fell in love with her. Ravana dispatched a golden deer disguised as Rama and Lakshmana to divert their attention away from Sita. He skillfully disguised himself as an elderly beggar and tricked Sita into leaving Lakshmana's protective ring. Taking advantage of the situation, Ravana showed his true self, kidnapped Sita, and took her away in his magical flying chariot to his dominion in Lanka (modern-day Sri Lanka).

Rama engaged in a bloody battle to free Sita from Ravana's grasp. He was assisted by the monkey god Hanuman and an army of monkeys and bears. After vanquishing Ravana and coming back to Ayodhya, Rama had to convince his subjects of Sita's purity, as they questioned her loyalty while she was being held captive.

Sita remained loyal to Rama throughout her struggle, so she made the decision to put herself through a trial by fire (*agni pariksha*) to establish her innocence and defend her honor. She made it through the trial unhurt, and her virtue was confirmed. However, Sita was exiled from Rama's realm after being pressured by his subjects, and she returned to the earth by entering its womb.

Sita's trial by fire.
https://commons.wikimedia.org/wiki/File:Sita%27s_ordeal_by_fire_(cropped).jpg

One of the holiest occasions in Hindu mythology, the marriage of Sita and Lord Rama, is commemorated every year by Hindus all over the world. Tradition has it that the union took place during the *Treta Yuga*, which is thought to have been some 1.2 million years ago.

Another reason Sita is well known is because of her constant love for Lord Rama and her unwavering sense of morality and decency. Sita endured many hardships in her lifetime, including being kidnapped by the demon king Ravana and living in exile with Lord Rama for a number of years, yet she never wavered in her love for him or her dedication to virtue.

Attributes and Symbolism

Sita is respected as a role model for women to follow and is frequently portrayed as a symbol of chastity, virtue, and devotion. She is frequently presented as a kind wife.

As social, cultural, and political settings altered over time, the concept of Sita also changed. In some regions of India, Sita is revered as a fertility and agricultural goddess who bestows favors and wealth upon her believers. The tale of her life is utilized to further moral and ethical principles in other cultures, where she is regarded as a representation of purity. Modern feminist and anti-colonialist movements in India and elsewhere are inspired by Sita, who has emerged as a cultural icon. Some academics contend that Sita's tale might be interpreted as a criticism of the patriarchy and praise women's independence and resiliency in the face of adversity.

Bhumi

Bhumi, sometimes spelled as Bhudevi and Vasundhara, is a Hindu deity linked to fertility and the earth. She is revered as the mother of all creatures and is bestowed with abundant gifts of food, water, and other natural resources. Bhumi is one of the Sapta Matrika, a group of seven mother goddesses revered in Hinduism and frequently grouped together in temples and shrines all over India.

Bhumi is shown as a lovely woman with a contented look. She is frequently depicted sitting or standing on a lotus or tortoise to represent her connection to the earth. She wears green attire, which stands for growth and nature. She wields a mace, a lotus, a plow, and a conch shell in her four arms, each of which stands for a distinct facet of her authority and influence.

Origin and Meaning

Bhumi is frequently seen in Hindu imagery alongside plants that represent development and fertility, such as fruit trees and lotus flowers. Additionally, she is connected to the positive hues of green and yellow. She is sometimes portrayed cradling an infant child, signifying her function as a nurturing and caring mother.

The veneration of Bhumi has changed in style and significance over the years as Hinduism evolved. She is regarded as a local deity in various parts of India. She is revered in other regions as part of a broader pantheon of deities, and elaborate rites and ceremonies have been passed down by practitioners through the ages to honor her.

Attributes and Symbolism

Bhumi has been worshiped since the early Vedic era in ancient India. There are several references to the earth and its significance as a source of life in the Vedas. As a representation of the earth's natural energies and a representation of the divine power that underlies all of creation, Bhumi was probably worshiped in early Vedic rites.

The tale of Bhumi's birth is one of the most well-known tales connected with her. Hindu mythology claims the gods went to Lord Vishnu to request his assistance in defeating the demon Hiranyaksha, who had taken the earth and concealed it in the ocean's depths. In order to fight the demon, Vishnu took the form of a boar and dove into the ocean. He was able to save the earth and put it back in its proper position in the cosmos. During this titanic conflict, Bhumi is supposed to have sprouted from Vishnu's sweat, signifying the close relationship between the earth and the deity Lord Vishnu.

Bhumi's role in the world's creation is the subject of another well-known myth. This story states that the god Brahma, who is credited with creating the universe, asked Bhumi for help in creating the material world. Her influence is evident in the diversity and abundance of the natural world, as well as the fact that she provided the raw materials and natural resources required to form the land, oceans, and skies.

Bhumi's significance increased throughout time as Hinduism developed and broadened to encompass a variety of gods, goddesses, and celestial creatures. Her importance in the Hindu pantheon increased, along with her position as a motherly figure and a source of fertility and abundance.

In order to encourage environmental sustainability and safeguard the earth's natural resources, there has been a resurgence in interest in the worship of Bhumi in recent years.

Conclusion

To sum up, the Hindu pantheon is abundant with a wide range of goddesses that represent various virtues and powers. They continue to have a significant influence on Hindu society today. Each goddess has her own mythology, symbolism, and rituals. From the fierce and guarding Durga to the caring and compassionate Parvati, these goddesses serve as role models for their followers, reminding them of the strength and beauty of the feminine divine.

The worship and adoration of goddesses will surely continue to be an essential component of this age-old and dynamic religion.

Chapter 6: Krishna the Supreme

Krishna, also known as *Kṛṣṇa* in Sanskrit, is one of the most revered and beloved divinities in India. He is worshiped as the eighth incarnation of Vishnu. Over the years, numerous bhakti cults have produced a large amount of religious art, with Krishna serving as their main religious icon.

Krishna's story is primarily drawn from the *Mahabharata*, a Hindu epic, and its 5th-century appendix, the *Harivamsa*, as well as the Puranas. Krishna, the son of Vasudeva and Devaki, was born into the Yadava family.

In order to kill the evil king Kamsa, Krishna and his brother Balarama made their way back to Mathura. The Yadavas, an ancient people who all worshiped Krishna, were then driven to the western shore of Kathiawar, where they constructed Dvaraka, the location of their court. Prince Krishna wed Princess Rukmini, although he also had other spouses.

Krishna's story has had a significant impact on Indian culture, inspiring many forms of art, literature, and music. His teachings on devotion and morality, as expressed in the Bhagavad Gita, a Hindu scripture of the *Mahabharata*, remain influential today.

The Birth Story of Lord Krishna

Lord Vishnu was incarnated as Krishna to protect dharma and spread peace on earth. Because of his dark skin, he was given the name Krishna, which in Sanskrit means "the color of night." Krishna is depicted as a charming boy who plays the flute. He has sparkling eyes, a black or blue complexion, and a celestial shine. The birth of Krishna was a significant event in the history of Hinduism, as the young Krishna was destined to shape the spiritual fate of mankind.

Krishna's birth narrative features his parents, Devaki and Vasudeva, as well as his harsh maternal uncle, King Kamsa. King Kamsa arranged Devaki's marriage with Vasudeva, and during their marriage ceremony, Aakash Vani, a medium for the gods, proclaimed that Kamsa would be killed by Devaki's eighth son. Upon hearing this, Kamsa attempted to kill Devaki with his sword.

Devaki and Vasudeva were devoted and eager to raise children. Unfortunately, Krishna's birth occurred while his mother was in jail. Her evil brother, who was egotistical and power-hungry, had imprisoned her and her husband.

When Krishna was born as Devaki's eighth child, Kamsa was determined to eliminate him. Devaki carried her eighth child in her womb for a year, and on the midnight of Ashtami (the eighth day of the sixth month), she gave birth to Krishna amidst heavy rainfall. Despite being imprisoned, Devaki and Vasudeva prayed for mercy and protection for their child.

In a miraculous turn of events, Vasudeva's chains broke, and the doors to their cell opened on their own. To protect their child from Kasma's wrath, Devaki embraced her child for one last goodbye before entrusting him to Vasudeva, who rushed toward Gokul with Krishna. Along the way, Vasudeva encountered rising waters in the River Yamuna and saw baskets on the riverbank. He placed the youngster in one of the baskets and carried it on his head.

The water level in the river was steadily rising when Vasudeva entered it due to a storm. Then, all of a sudden, the water level began to fall, and a big snake by the name of Shesha came to their aid. At first, Vasudeva was frightened, but he soon realized the snake was there to help him cross the river safely with Krishna. The snake protected the child from the rain and kept his hood spread over Vasudeva until they reached the shore.

Vasudeva and Devaki, before the birth of Krishna, were astonished to see that Yashoda, Nanda's wife (Nanda was a chief and would later become Krishna's foster father), had recently given birth to a baby girl when they arrived at his home. However, their arrival also brought great joy to the household since Vasudeva, Nanda's cousin, had returned after many years. Yashoda's heart broke as soon as she heard Vasudeva tell the couple the tale of his misery. She resolved to save their eighth son at any cost and asked Vasudeva if she could switch her girl with his son so that

Kamsa would not become suspicious.

This grand gesture from Yashoda took Vasudeva aback, and he was overcome with tears. He carried the young girl to Mathura in the basket. As soon as he entered the prison, the doors were locked, and the shackles were placed around him once more. The guards were awakened by the girl's crying, and they immediately alerted Kamsa about the eighth birth. As anticipated, Kamsa arrived and took the infant from Devaki, threatening to kill both of them. However, the infant girl abruptly disappeared into the sky and changed into a deity. From above, she warned Kamsa that his destroyer was being raised in Gokul and that his death was imminent.

At Nanda's house, the child was named Krishna and was raised by Yashoda and Nanda as their own. They showered him with love and care, just like they did with Balarama, the elder half-brother of Krishna.

Putana's Unsuccessful Attempt to Murder Baby Krishna

After learning that Devaki's eighth child had survived, Kamsa was distressed and sought a way to kill the baby boy. Putana, a demonic being with a terrifying visage, was instructed by Kamsa to execute all infants in the kingdom under the age of ten days to ensure that Krishna was killed. Because it would boost her reputation and instill fear in others, Putana was eager to accept the assignment. She killed every baby she could find while moving from village to village until she arrived in the community where Krishna lived. There, she discovered information about a unique youngster. She already knew that killing Krishna wouldn't be simple because he wasn't a typical kid.

Putana changed into a lovely lady to trick the villagers and Krishna's foster parents. She asked Yashoda if she could feed the boy, and Yashoda agreed. However, she would have said no if she had known that the stranger had injected lethal snake venom into her breasts. Putana brought Krishna outside and offered him milk that was poisoned. But Putana soon felt as if she was being suffocated by Krishna's strong grip. Krishna held onto Putana even after she changed into a demon to frighten him.

Putana attempted to fly upward to convince the child to let her go, but Krishna drained the life from her and caused her to crash to the ground. The small child was joyfully playing on the demon's body when the shocked townspeople discovered him.

Lord Krishna's Childhood

Krishna's time in Gokul is an essential part of his story. As an infant, Krishna captured the hearts of the *gopis*, the cowherd girls of the village, with his mischievous pranks and miraculous feats, such as killing demons and other things that were beyond the capabilities of ordinary mortals.

Krishna's charm only increased as he grew into a youth. His melodic flute-playing would draw the *gopis*, including the beautiful Radha, the wife of a *gopa* (a cowherd), out of their homes to dance with him in the moonlight. Radha was held dear by Krishna, who remained devoted to him. According to a well-known story, Krishna even saved the villagers from the wrath of Lord Indra, who caused torrential rain in the village. He raised Govardhan Hill with his little finger and used it as an umbrella to shelter the villagers from the deluge.

Krishna's divine power and benevolent nature soon became apparent to all. His uncle Kamsa, who had imprisoned his mother, was still determined to eliminate him. Many assassins were dispatched by Kamsa to kill Krishna, but none were successful. Ultimately, Krishna and his brother Balarama made their way back to Mathura, where they executed Kamsa and established law. Following their triumph, Krishna and the Yadavas (Krishna's clan) relocated to Dvaraka, which is now in Gujarat. He took eight wives there, including Rukmini, a stunning princess from the Vidarbha Kingdom. Ashtabharya is the collective name for his wives.

Kamsa's Failed Attempts to Kill Krishna Led to His Own Demise

Despite Kamsa's repeated attempts to eliminate Krishna, he remained unsuccessful. To get rid of Krishna and Balarama, Kamsa and his servant came up with a fresh strategy. The brothers accepted an invitation to watch a wrestling match in Mathura. They also faced off against two of Kamsa's most powerful wrestlers in the contest, whom they easily defeated.

Kamsa was furious by the defeat and gave the order for his soldiers to kill Krishna and Balarama. However, Krishna stopped them by leaping into the audience and grabbing Kamsa's crown. He then dragged Kamsa by his hair into the wrestling ring. Kamsa challenged Krishna to a wrestling contest in an effort to show off his might, but Kamsa was killed by one strike from Krishna's hand. After Kamsa's death, Krishna set Devaki and Vasudeva, his biological parents, free. This story teaches us that truth and goodness always emerge victorious in the end.

Krishna and Kaliya

Krishna lived a simple life in the village. Each morning, Lord Krishna would take his cows to the river so they could graze. After a while, tragedy stuck. The cows started dying suddenly. And it wasn't just those cows, but everything surrounding the river was poisoned, including the birds that flew over it and the marine life. No one knew what had happened, but Krishna was determined to find out. Krishna discovered that the ten-headed serpent Kaliya lived in the river and was responsible for poisoning the animals that depended upon the river for survival.

Krishna addressed the enormous serpent and pleaded with him to stop tainting the water. Being wicked and obstinate, Kaliya objected. So, Krishna dove into the hazardous water and danced on Kaliya's head.

The villagers gathered around, anxious for the incredible Krishna, but they were stunned at the sight. As time passed, Krishna became heavier and heavier as he danced on top of all ten of Kaliya's heads. Soon, the weight became unbearable for the ten-headed serpent. The dancing actually left an imprint of Krishna's feet on one of Kaliya's heads. Kaliya's wife cried out to Krishna and pleaded for forgiveness. Her cries moved Krishna, and on the condition that Kaliya and his wife cross the river and leave, he would spare Kaliya's life.

Why Is Lord Krishna Called Ranchod?

One of the many names used to refer to Lord Krishna is Ranchod, which has a fascinating origin story. In the time of the *Dvapara Yuga*, Krishna moved to Madhura to protect his Yadava clan from constant attacks by enemies. The Yadava dynasty was assaulted by the unstoppable demon Kalayavana, Jarasandha of Magadha, and other enemies. In order to save the Yadavas, Krishna built the majestic city of Dvaraka in the middle of the ocean and then moved the Yadavas there.

Krishna pretended to flee the battlefield when the men of Kalayavana pursued him. These men were closely followed by the demon. Kalayavana was lured by Krishna into a cave, the latter of whom pretended to flee the battlefield. In the cave, Muchukunda was meditating. Muchukunda, a ruler from the *Treta Yuga* and an ancestor of Lord Rama, had supported Indra in his conflict with the Asuras. Muchukunda sought a long stretch of uninterrupted sleep to revitalize himself after helping Indra win. Additionally, he demanded that anyone who woke him up be burned to ash. Indra granted his wish.

Krishna led Kalayavana into the cave where Muchukunda was sleeping, and Kalayavana accidentally woke him up. Muchukunda's glare burned Kalayavana to ashes. Thus, Lord Krishna earned the name Ranchod, which means "one who flees from the battlefield." This incident showcases Krishna's cleverness and his ability to protect his people from powerful enemies.

Krishna and His Love for Butter

Krishna had an insatiable craving for butter. Gokul, the village where he resided, was well supplied with butter, milk, and curds. Every chance he got, Krishna would take a pot of butter from either his mother or another villager. To keep Krishna from stealing the butter pots, the *gopis* and village mothers began to tie them to the ceiling. They hoped that the small, young Krishna would not be able to reach the pots and that their dairy products would be safe.

However, the cunning Krishna and his companions managed to get the pots by standing on each other's shoulders or rearranging the ceiling tiles. And if that did not give them what they wanted, they would throw stones at the pots and catch the butter with their mouths as it poured down.

When the *gopis* found out, they complained to Krishna's foster mother, Yashoda. She made a commitment to correct him, but instead of doing as he was told, Krishna robbed the *gopis* of their clothing while they were taking a bath in the river. He promised to return their clothes if they vowed to quit whining to his mother.

Unable to correct her unruly son, Yashoda chained Krisna to a large staff. Krishna was able to release himself by moving into the forest with the staff. He became wedged between two trees that were near to one another, but he pulled so hard that he uprooted both, releasing himself in the process. When Yashoda saw her little boy's strength, she realized that he was no ordinary child.

The Great War of Kurukshetra

Arjuna, a Pandava prince, learned to rely on Krishna as a confidant and friend. However, a terrible conflict was brewing between the Pandavas (five legendary brothers) and the Kauravas, the descendants of Kuru, a legendary Indian king. The two sides prepared for war, and Krishna, who wanted to avoid bloodshed, attempted to mediate between the parties. He proposed that the Kauravas grant the Pandavas a small piece of land, but Dhritarashtra (the father of the Kauravas in this story) refused, as he was determined to crush the Pandavas once and for all.

As the situation escalated, Krishna offered to help the Pandavas, but he refused to fight himself, as he believed that violence would only lead to more suffering. Lord Krishna spoke the well-known Bhagavad Gita. He proclaimed, "I am the exclusive creator of this universe, and I can effortlessly destroy my enemies with my 'Sudarshan Chakra' at will. However, I want to educate future generations about the significance of Karma, the act of performing one's duties. One must carry out their duties without being attached to the outcome and avoid being driven by the result. Instead, they should relish the journey of reaching their destination."

Krishna allowed Arjuna to choose between his presence and the loan of his army. Arjuna chose Krishna's wisdom over his troops, recognizing that his advice was worth more than any army. Despite Krishna's best efforts, war was inevitable, and it resulted in the tragic loss of life.

Following the conflict, Krishna went to see Gandhari, Dhritarashtra's aunt. She had lost one hundred of her sons to the battle. She was grieving and angry and cursed Krishna, as she believed he could have prevented the bloodshed. She said that he and his entire dynasty, the Yadavas, would perish within thirty-six years, a curse that came true.

Lord Krishna in Art

Since the 5th century BCE, Hindus have revered Krishna. In Bengal and Udupi, India, in particular, he is regarded as the supreme Hindu deity. Many celebrations are held in his honor, with Krishna Janmashtami being the most well known. On this day, devotees fast for twenty-four hours and present milk-based desserts to the infant Krishna. Wicks are lit at midnight after being steeped in butter as part of the ceremony to celebrate the birth of Krishna.

Krishna is frequently pictured in art as having dark blue or black skin, donning a yellow garment, and sporting a peacock feather in his hair. He frequently appears with cows and plays the flute, a nod to his earlier days as a cowherd. Krishna is also remembered for possessing the Kaumodaki (Lord Vishnu's mace) and the chakra discus of Vajranabha (a Yadava king), both of which were gifts from Agni, the fire god.

The numerous components of Krishna's personality come from several deities. In the 5th century BCE, Vasudeva-Krishna (as in the son of Vasudeva) was worshiped, while Krishna the cowherd was revered as a pastoral deity. In the end, the two came together to form Narayana (an avatar of Vishnu). With Krishna's adolescent liaisons with *gopis* being regarded as indications of a loving interplay between god and the human soul, Krishna's worship also offers a distinctive understanding of the parallels between divine and human love.

Due to the numerous legends surrounding Krishna's existence, there are several paintings and sculptures representing him in various settings. The infant Krishna is frequently portrayed crawling on his hands and knees or dancing merrily while holding a butterball in his lap. Krishna is also shown as a divine lover playing the flute while surrounded by prostrate *gopis*. The image of Krishna being worshiped is one of the most well-known ones.

Lord Krishna: Personal Life

In accordance with popular belief, Sri (Lord) Krishna had sons from each of his eight primary wives. At the time that he killed the demon Narakasura, who was a harsh ruler, it is said that he had 16,100 wives, most of whom came from the Palace of Narakasura. This is interpreted as a manifestation of Sri Krishna's compassion for people who were victimized by outdated social mores and cultural norms.

Rukmini, Satyabhama, Jambavati, Kalindi, Mitravinda, Nagnajiti, Lakshmana, and Bhadra were Sri Krishna's eight primary wives. All ten of Sri Krishna's sons were born to one of these eight queens.

According to an earlier version of the Bhagavata Purana, Sri Krishna is also said to have had a girl named Charumati with Rukmini.

Conclusion

Krishna's life and teachings have been a source of inspiration for people of all ages and backgrounds. His story teaches us about the importance of love, friendship, devotion, and sacrifice. Krishna's message is universal and relevant today as we strive to find meaning and purpose in our lives.

Krishna's life was full of challenges, but he faced them with grace and wisdom. His teachings continue to provide guidance to people seeking to live a life of purpose, meaning, and service. Through his life and teachings, Krishna has left an indelible mark on Hinduism and the world, and his legacy will continue to inspire generations to come.

Chapter 7: Ganesha, Lord of Luck

Ganesha, also known as Ganesh, is referred to as the Remover of Obstacles. The story of his birth, of coming to life from Parvati's tears and being beheaded by his father, who replaced his head with that of an elephant, also gave him the title of the Lord of Luck and the Lord of New Beginnings. He is a revered and celebrated deity, and as the Lord of New Beginnings, he is often invoked at the beginning of religious ceremonies.

While some texts relate his origins to Shiva and Parvati, some traditions, in particular, the Ganapatya, believe Ganesha to be the Supreme Being. Aside from his most notable attribute, the elephant head, Ganesha is also known as the patron of knowledge, the arts, sciences, and wisdom. His avatar names include Ganapati, Vinayaka, and Pillaiyar.

Appearance

Ganesha

Pradeep Kumar Sharma, CC BY-SA 4.0 <https://creativecommons.org/licenses/by-sa/4.0>, via Wikimedia Commons. Image has been cropped. https://commons.wikimedia.org/wiki/File:Lord-ganesha-22.jpg

The Ganesha Purana, written somewhere between 1100 and 1400 CE, offers the greatest insight into Ganesha. He is depicted with an elephant head in texts. Although the story of Shiva replacing his head with that of an elephant is the most popular, other explanations exist.

Some texts suggest that Ganesha was simply born with an elephant head. Another suggests that Ganesha was born by Shiva's laughter. His form made Shiva jealous, as he considered him too physically alluring. In response, Shiva gave his son the head of an elephant and a protruding belly. Certain texts also state that Ganesha had five elephant heads instead of one head.

Ganesha has been regularly depicted with a single tusk, and mythological texts state that the other tusk was broken. As such, he is also known as Ekadanta, one-tusked, although this name is also attributed to his second incarnation. In his second reincarnation, Ganesha emerges as Ekadanta and travels upon a mouse to defeat the demon Madasur. In some imagery, Ganesha holds his broken tusk in one hand.

Ganesha's round belly became a rather distinctive attribute and can be seen in pictorial depictions and statues that emerged between the 4th and 6th centuries CE. The feature is important enough to have two of Ganesha's incarnations named after it: Lambodara and Mahodara, meaning "hanging belly" and "great belly," respectively. Ganesha's belly is also symbolic, as it is believed to hold all of the universes, the past, present, and future.

Many gods and goddesses in Indian mythology are portrayed with more than two arms, and Ganesha is no different, although the number of his arms varies based on texts, with his more famous depictions having up to sixteen arms. The most common depictions, particularly in the Puranas, have four arms, although up to twenty arms can be seen in certain depictions between the 9th and 10th centuries. Ganesha also often appears with a serpent, sometimes wrapped around his neck, ankles, or stomach, or as a sacred thread held in one hand. Sometimes, Ganesha sits on a throne.

Ganesha's forehead features a third eye, with three lines placed horizontally across the forehead, along with a crescent moon. The depiction of the moon is consistent with one of Ganesha's incarnations, Bhalchandra, or "moon on the forehead." Ganesha's depictions appear in various colors, which stems from the specific text in which he is mentioned. He is commonly seen in the color red. However, his other forms have also shown him in the color white, and his Ekadanta form is often shown in the color blue.

Ganesha's entire appearance holds symbolic meaning as well. The elephant head is a mark of his title as the Remover of Obstacles since elephants remove obstacles in forests to create a path for others to follow. It also stands for the wisdom and intellect one must possess and exercise in life to succeed. Ganesha has large ears, which signify the importance of listening, and his trunk holds everything in existence in the universe.

Etymology

Ganesha's name has its roots in Sanskrit, with the joining of the words *gana* and *isha*, which mean "multitude" and "lord," respectively. Ganas is also the name of the troops of Shiva, and so Ganesha is taken to mean the Lord of the Ganas, which is also noted in his alternate name Ganapati, with *pati* meaning "ruler." Known names of Ganesha's avatars include the following:

- Ganapati
- Vinayaka
- Vighnaraja
- Vighneshwara
- Dvaimatura
- Ganadhipa
- Ekadanta
- Heramba
- Lambodara
- Gajanana

The name Vinayaka is often mentioned in Puranic texts. The eight Ganesha temples in Maharashtra, known collectively as Ashtavinayaka, are named after Vinayaka. The names Vighnaraja and Vighneshwara both signify his title as the Remover of Obstacles, as Vighnaraja means one who removes obstacles and Vighneshwara the one who creates obstacles.

Another common name for Ganesha is taken from the Tamil language. Pillaiyar translates to "noble child." However, taken from the words *pallu* or *pella*, it can also mean elephant tooth or tusk, obviously denoting Ganesha's unique appearance.

Features

Much like other gods of mythology, there are many unique features and attributes associated with Ganesha that signify his role in the cosmic order. These range from the titles he has been given, such as the Remover of Obstacles, to other notable and symbolic features that people should follow to lead wise and successful lives.

Remover of Obstacles

The title of Remover of Obstacles may signify many roles. It may be symbolic, stemming from his elephant form since elephants create paths for others to follow. As Ganesha is also known for his wisdom, the title also signifies his role in creating paths in the spiritual world. However, his role is not simply to remove obstacles. Ganesha places obstacles in the paths of those who deviate from the righteous path or seek to create chaos or evil. This also highlights why Ganesha is celebrated and worshiped at the beginning of any ritual, as invoking him will remove obstacles from people's spiritual path and allow the ritual to continue without any issues.

Symbolically, Ganesha represents the power in each person to overcome the obstacles that face them. Yet his role as the remover of obstacles is not split from his role as the creator of obstacles. In essence, this can mean that moving astray from one's path can create obstacles in life, whereas staying on the right path and practicing wisdom and the use of intellect can keep one away from the challenges of life.

In other interpretations, Ganesha's role as the creator of obstacles is to create perseverance in life. Obstacles allow people to develop strength to face difficult moments in life. As a remover of obstacles, Ganesha practices complete control over disturbing impulses that, if acted on, could lead to the creation of obstacles in one's path. Thus, such obstacles are removed by practicing self-control and by the use of wisdom and strength.

Buddhi (Intelligence)

As the Lord of Letters and Learning, one of Ganesha's most noticeable attributes is his intelligence. Buddhi, or intellect, is a concept that is present in the stories of Ganesha that demonstrate his love and desire for intelligence and cleverness. As such, Ganesha is often referred to as one possessing universal intelligence, or *mahat-tattva*. Among the non-permanent realities that are created and destroyed, intelligence is considered the highest form, and Ganesha, as its possessor, is held in high esteem.

Intelligence in living beings is seen as the culmination of the self, Shiva, and of nature, Parvati. Ganesha, who was born to Shiva and Parvati, is a mixture of their respective traits and can thus possess supreme intelligence. His intellect also relates to his title of Remover of Obstacles, as a great level of intellect is required to carry on through life while removing unnecessary obstructions from one's path.

Along with buddhi, another feature attributed to Ganesha is perfection, siddhi. More specifically, he grants perfection. Hindus believe that one should not pray for materialistic things but rather for intelligence and perfection. Siddhi is most aptly achieved when one receives something before they have a chance to desire it, achieving true perfection. For example, someone who is able to achieve success in life, such as wealth, would not harbor a desire for more money. However, when a desire is expressed and not fulfilled, it shows a lack of siddhi and may also indicate a lack of buddhi. The worship of Ganesha, therefore, brings the qualities of perfection and intellect to the worshiper, who is then able to deal with the challenges of life.

Om

The Om symbol.
https://commons.wikimedia.org/wiki/File:Aum_Om_black.svg

Om is a Hindu mantra with which Ganesha is identified. Ganesha is seen as the personification of the primal sound. Some texts refer to him as the Supreme Being, the culmination of the Trimurti, holding air and fire, the sun and the moon, and the combined three worlds of heaven, earth, and hell. Ganesha, as the possessor or personification of Om, refers to his mastery over all this.

Ganesha is often referred to as Omkara (one with the form of Om) since he manifests it. Many texts and those who practice the worship of Ganesha note that the outline of his body matches the letter that is used to refer to Om. As the personification of all of the cosmos, Ganesha holds great importance and is therefore referred to as a lord equal to the Trimurti.

The mantra that is said to Ganesha is "Om gam ganapataye namaha," which first addresses the primordial sound Om over which Ganesha has complete control and which translates to "wake up." *Gam* and *ganapataye* both refer to Ganesha, and *namaha* offers the reciters salutations and worship to Ganesha. It is also a calling for Ganesha to help the reciter as the remover of obstacles and help them unlock their chakra, or energy centers of the body, and achieve stability in life, over which Ganesha is also lord. The mantra helps tame one's internal anxiety, boosts physical health, and opens the door to wisdom and intellect, which can then lead to better decision-making in life rather than the anxiety one was experiencing.

First Chakra

The Muladhara, or the first chakra, is where Ganesha is believed to reside. This is the root chakra. In the Muladhara, the manifestation and expression of the divine force rest, and Ganesha presides over it. Associated with the earth element, the root chakra is found in one's physical form, namely in the body and in the bones. Ganesha rules the root chakra with his elephant head, his portly belly, and his human form. As the ruler of the Muladhara, Ganesha guides the connection between living beings and their bodies.

The cosmic energies received by the body come through the seven chakras, and the root chakra forms the base of these energies. It is located near the base of the spine and is often associated with the act of secretion. A strong root chakra indicates a strong base, survival, and the ability to stand up for oneself. Without it, one loses their sense and feeling of belonging, creating a weak outlook on life.

Thus, Ganesha is the source of stability, belonging, health, and wealth in the lives of those who master the root chakra. It is also said that Ganesha dwells in the spinal plexus of everybody, which means he is with everyone, offering his support, intellect, and wisdom to those who are able to master the Muladhara. Ganesha also acts as a guide to all the other chakras, thereby guiding the manifestation of one's life and success.

Stories of Ganesha

There are many stories that relate to Ganesha. Many of these signify his attributes, such as his mastery over the root chakra or his wisdom and intellect. Some stories differ in the way they are told. Regardless, they provide insight into the role and significance of Ganesha in the greater cosmic order.

Ganesha's Birth

There are several stories about Ganesha's birth, and many of them seem to vary on certain facts regarding how he came to be and, in particular, how he came to have a single tusk. One story suggests that Ganesha was born from a cloth doll that was brought to life by Parvati's tears after Shiva refused her a child, although a similar story suggests that while Parvati did make Ganesha out of cloth, she asked Shiva to bring him to life.

A more well-known story regarding his birth does not relate to Parvati's desire for a child at all. Instead, Ganesha came to be when Parvati, who wished to bathe without being interrupted by Shiva, conjured Ganesha by kneading the dirt that lay about her and shaping it into a child. The child then came to life. He was assigned to guard the way to where she bathed and to let no one in. When Shiva arrived, he saw a handsome boy who refused him entry. So, he cut the boy's head off in anger. Upon seeing Parvati's sorrow, he vowed to make Ganesha whole again and set off in search of a replacement. The only thing he found was an elephant's head, which was placed on Ganesha's body.

Ganesha is sometimes referred to as only Parvati's son since he was born from one parent. However, he is most commonly referred to as the son of both Parvati and Shiva.

Although there are many stories about how Ganesha only has one tusk, the simplest is that one of his tusks broke off when Shiva placed the elephant's head onto Ganesha's body. Ganesha held on to the broken tusk in one hand. However, other stories differ from this and narrate a different sequence of events that led to the broken tusk.

The Broken Tusk

In one story, Ganesha, as the patron of letters and the arts, sat down to write the *Mahabharata*. This epic poem is one of the longest in existence, and as Ganesha wrote it, the pen he was using broke in his hand. To not let his writing be interrupted, Ganesha is believed to have broken off his tusk and used it as a pen. This sacrifice for an artistic purpose reinforces Ganesha's role as the Lord of Letters and shows his dedication to creating something, even if it came at a personal cost.

Another story presents a different lesson, one of loyalty, and also presents the source of the name Ekadanta. In this story, Shiva asked Ganesha to guard over him while he rested and to allow no stranger to pass through. Ganesha took his post while Shiva slept and stayed true to his task. While Shiva was sleeping, a Brahmin (a warrior) came to visit him, known as Parashuram. Ganesha did not know this warrior and so turned him away. Angered at being refused and also not knowing who Ganesha was, Parashuram began to fight with Ganesha. In his anger, the warrior threw his ax at Ganesha's head, which Ganesha stopped with his tusk, breaking it in the process. Still, he did not let the warrior pass. As for Parashuram, he realized his mistake and felt sorry for what he had done. He asked Shiva for forgiveness, which was granted. This story shows Ganesha's devotion to his assigned duty and his father.

Ganesha's Wisdom

There are many stories that narrate Ganesha's wisdom. One such story begins with Ganesha's conflict with his younger brother Karthikeya, also known as Skanda. The conflict began when the brothers happened upon a unique fruit in the forest. Naturally, each wanted it all to himself and refused to share it with the other. So, they decided to take the matter up with their parents and headed to Mount Kailash.

Shiva immediately recognized the fruit as one possessing great powers; it could grant its eater immortality and great knowledge but could only be consumed by the one with the right to eat it. To resolve their conundrum, Shiva proposed a challenge to the brothers, which they accepted. He asked them both to make three rounds of the world. Whoever finished first would possess the right to consume the fruit of knowledge and immortality.

While Skanda immediately took his pet peacock and began riding around the world, Ganesha took a moment to consider what Shiva had said and realized the trick in the challenge. Instead of attempting to go around all of the created universes, he made three rounds around Shiva and Parvati. Satisfied and impressed by Ganesha's wisdom, Shiva made him the rightful owner of the fruit.

Ganesha's Curse of the Moon

Ganesha's tale about his curse of the moon also relates to his broken tusk. It begins with Ganesha's return journey from a feast thrown by the god of wealth, Kubera. Ganesha had eaten well at the feast, and his mount, a mouse, was having trouble carrying the extra weight. Here, some tales deviate, stating that Ganesha's extra weight made the mouse topple. Other stories suggest that as Ganesha made his journey, a snake crossed his path, and the mouse ran off, causing Ganesha to fall off. His stomach split open, emptying everything he had eaten at the feast.

Ganesha hastily stuffed everything back and took the serpent, tying it around his stomach to hold it in place. However, he heard the moon laughing at him, which angered Ganesha. He broke off one of his tusks and flung it at the moon, which immediately cracked. Ganesha cursed the moon, saying that it would never be whole again. In some versions, Ganesha cursed the moon to never be worshiped during the night of Ganesh Chaturthi. Thus, Ganesha lost his tusk, and the moon earned a permanent crater.

Worship

Thirteenth-century Ganesha statue.
Quadell, CC BY-SA 3.0 <http://creativecommons.org/licenses/by-sa/3.0/>, via Wikimedia Commons; https://commons.wikimedia.org/wiki/File:13th_century_Ganesha_statue.jpg

The worship of Ganesha is not limited to religious events but is a part of daily life for many Hindus. Since he is the Remover of Obstacles, he is often worshiped before the commencement of any undertaking, such as buying a new vehicle, starting a new business, or anything that signifies a new beginning.

Ganesh Chaturthi is an annual festival celebrated in the early fall in honor of Ganesha. The festival lasts ten days, and its beginning is marked by people bringing clay idols of Ganesha. At the end of the ten-day festival, on the day of Anata Chaturdashi, the idols are taken to a suitable body of water and immersed there to allow Ganesha to return home after staying with his devotees for the festival.

Additionally, temple worship of Ganesha is common, but he is portrayed differently based on the temple. He often appears as a subordinate deity (a second deity to the principal deity). In other instances, especially in temples dedicated to him, Ganesha is the principal deity.

Chapter 8: Tales from the *Mahabharata*

The *Mahabharata* is a significant Indian epic and is regarded as one of the longest epic poems ever written. It was initially composed in Sanskrit and is thought to have been written by the sage Vyasa. The epic is an essential component of Indian culture, and literature, art, and philosophy have been impacted by its tales, characters, and lessons for centuries.

The *Mahabharata* describes a war between two branches of the Kuru dynasty for control of the Kuru Kingdom. The five Pandava brothers' conflict with their Kaurava cousins, who seized control of their kingdom, is the central theme of the story. The eldest brother, Yudhishthira, is in charge of the Pandavas, who are regarded as the story's main characters. Duryodhana, the eldest brother, is in charge of the Kauravas.

The epic is supposedly set in the ancient Kuru Kingdom, which is said to be in what is now northern India's Haryana. The Kuru dynasty and its kings, including King Shantanu and his son Bhishma, are introduced at the beginning of the story. The plot then follows the Pandavas' lives and their conflicts with the Kauravas, which ultimately result in a terrible battle.

The *Mahabharata* explores a variety of philosophical and ethical topics in addition to telling the tale of a conflict between two families. Discussions of dharma (goodness), karma (activities and their results), and *moksha* (deliverance from the cycle of life and death) are all included in the epic. A discussion between the warrior Arjuna and his charioteer Krishna makes up the Bhagavad Gita, which is a chapter of the

Mahabharata. One of the most important Hindu teachings is the dialogue between Arjuna and Krishna, as it examines a number of spiritual and ethical ideas.

There are other storylines and subplots in the *Mahabharata* as well. The tale of Nala and Damayanti is one such tale that explores the concepts of love and trust. Another well-known story is the tale of Savitri and Satyavan, which is about loyalty and devotion.

The *Mahabharata* is not only a religious book; it is also a work of culture and history. It sheds light on the habits, traditions, and ideals of ancient Indian society. The epic depicts the numerous roles that women play in society, especially the formidable and powerful figure of Draupadi, the Pandava king's wife. The value of family, allegiance, and honor in Indian culture is also portrayed in it.

Satyavati and the Kuru Dynasty

King Shantanu and Satyavati.
https://commons.wikimedia.org/wiki/File:Santanu,_a_king_of_Hastinapura_in_the_Mahabharata,_saw_a_beautiful_woman_on_the_banks_of_the_river_Ganga.jpg

An essential figure in the epic *Mahabharata* was Satyavati. Born to be a fisherwoman, Satyavati was renowned for her extraordinary beauty and charisma. Her life is an amazing story of love and devotion.

Satyavati was the daughter of a fisherman named Dasharaja. Because of her father's occupation, she was given the name Matsyagandha, which translates to "one who smells of fish." Nevertheless, she was endowed with great beauty and grace despite coming from a lowly background.

One day, Satyavati drew Parashara's attention while she was escorting the great sage across the river. He asked her to spend the night with him. Initially reluctant, Satyavati consented on the condition that he would make her smell good forever. She got her wish.

Satyavati gave birth to a boy after their night together, and he was given the name Vyasa. Vyasa would later become a famous sage and pen the *Mahabharata*.

After some time, Satyavati wed King Shantanu of Hastinapur, who was captivated by her beauty and elegance. But they faced difficulties in their marriage. Chitrangada and Vichitravirya were the names of Satyavati and Shantanu's two children. Vichitravirya became the only heir to the kingdom after Chitrangada's early death.

When Vichitravirya was of marriageable age, Satyavati made arrangements for his union with the king of Kashi's daughters, Ambika and Ambalika. However, Vichitravirya passed very quickly after the wedding and left no heir. As a result, there was no one to take the throne, which caused a crisis in the country.

Satyavati requested the assistance of Vyasa, her child from her union with Parashara, to preserve the survival of the Kuru dynasty. She asked him to have children with Ambika and Ambalika so that the Kuru dynasty's legacy would live on. Satyavati gave Vyasa the order to conceive Ambika while she was in her reproductive cycle. When they first met, Ambika's discomfort with Vyasa's dark skin caused her to close her eyes. She thus gave birth to a robust, blind boy who went on to become the ancestor of the Kauravas. Satyavati deemed his condition to be inappropriate for a monarch, and she requested that Vyasa perform a similar act with her younger daughter-in-law, Ambalika. But when Ambalika saw Vyasa, she grew frightened and gave birth to a thin infant. Thus, Pandu, the pallid one, and Dhritarashtra, the blind monarch, entered the universe.

Satyavati was essential to the founding and survival of the Kuru dynasty. Her descendants carried on her heritage by taking part in the epic battle of Kurukshetra.

Pandu and Dhritarashtra

In the *Mahabharata*, the two brothers named Pandu and Dhritarashtra had a significant impact on the events that led to the War of Kurukshetra.

Dhritarashtra was Pandu's older brother and was born blind. Due to his disability, Pandu was chosen to rule Hastinapura, the Kuru kingdom's capital.

Duryodhana, the major adversary of the *Mahabharata*, was one of Dhritarashtra's one hundred sons. He was married to Gandhari, who blindfolded herself so she could understand her husband's pain.

Dhritarashtra.
Ramanarayanadatta astri, CC0, via Wikimedia Commons;
https://commons.wikimedia.org/wiki/File:Dhritrashtra.jpg

Pandu, the younger brother, ruled for a time. One day, he was in the forest, enjoying the wildlife and the sounds of nature. All of a sudden, he heard the noise of a wild animal. He shot an arrow toward the sound, hitting a sage who had turned into a deer to engage in lovemaking. He curses Pandu, saying that he will die if he ever has sex. Pandu went into the forest with his wives, leaving the throne to Dhritarashtra.

The Conflict between the Pandava Brothers and Their Cousins, the Kauravas

The battle between the Pandavas and Kauravas.
https://commons.wikimedia.org/wiki/File:The_Pandava_brothers%27_nephew_Abhimanyu_battles_the_Kaurava_brother_Duhshasana,_from_a_manuscript_of_the_Mahabharata.jpg

The greatest fight in the *Mahabharata* is between the five Pandava brothers and their relatives, the Kauravas. The rivalry between the two lineages of the Kuru dynasty, which were descendants of the fabled King Kuru, was the cause of the conflict. The battle is a complicated tale encompassing a number of elements, including resentment, greed, pride, and power.

King Pandu was the father of the five Pandavas. But how did Pandu have five sons if he would die after having intercourse? A wise sage accepted their mother Kunti's yearning to call upon the gods' favor to have children. She invoked the gods Dharmaraja, Vayu, and Indra to give birth to her three sons, Yudhishthira, Bhima, and Arjuna. Madri, Pandu's other wife, prayed to the Ashvinis (Hindu twin gods that are associated with medicine, health, dawn, as well as the sciences) to help her conceive her two sons, Nakula and Sahadeva. Pandu eventually had sex with Madri and died soon afterward. Madri, ashamed at what had happened, committed suicide, leaving Kunti to raise the five sons on her own.

Kunti raised them in the capital alongside their cousins, the Kauravas. However, the eldest Kaurava, Duryodhana, refused to accept them as his family. He hated the Pandavas, and this hatred spread to the other Kauravas.

Several schemes to hurt or kill the Pandavas were developed by Duryodhana, which included poisoning their food, drowning them in a river, and burning them in a house of wax. Duryodhana believed the fire had killed them, but the brothers lived, having been forewarned of the plot.

News of the Pandavas' existence eventually reached their uncle's ears, and he welcomed them back to the kingdom with open arms. But Duryodhana, who was now the recognized heir, did not want them to return, as he knew questions about inheritance would be raised. Dhritarashtra knew it would not be right to cut the Pandavas out entirely, so he kept the capital and its surrounding lands for himself and his son and gave desolate lands to the Pandavas.

It was challenging, but the Pandavas were able to build their kingdom into something amazing. Duryodhana, who was greatly influenced by his uncle, Shakuni, decided to play a dice game with his eldest cousin, Yudhishthira. The dice Duryodhana used was magical, allowing him to win every time. First, he cheated Yudhishthira out of his wealth and kingdom. Then, Yudhishthira bet his brothers, himself, and even his wife, making the family slaves to Duryodhana. in which he cheated and gained the kingdom.

Duryodhana humiliated the Pandavas, causing Dhritarashtra to finally intervene, giving everything back to the Pandavas. But Duryodhana threw a fit and threatened to kill himself if he wasn't allowed to play one more game with the Pandavas. This time, the loser would be sent to live in the forest for twelve years and spend the thirteenth year in disguise. If their cover was blown during the thirteenth year, the cycle would begin again. Thanks to the magical dice, Duryodhana won, and the Pandavas were exiled.

The Pandavas spent their time wisely, gathering supplies and an army to take the capital by force if needed. When their time was up, they returned to Hastinapura, asking for their former kingdom back. Duryodhana, who was now the king, was unwilling to divide his kingdom. Krishna intervened, asking for Duryodhana to give up five villages, but he still refused. A war was unavoidable. According to tradition, millions of troops and fighters perished during the eighteen-day Kurukshetra War, which also claimed the lives of some significant *Mahabharata* figures, including Bhishma, Drona, Karna, and many others. The Pandavas ultimately triumphed, and Yudhishthira was anointed king of Hastinapura.

The struggle between good and evil and the victory of dharma (righteousness) over adharma (unrighteousness) are represented by the war between the Pandavas and the Kauravas. The narrative is also full of lessons, and it has served as an example and a source of inspiration for individuals of all ages.

The Bhagavad Gita

A seven-hundred-verse Hindu scripture known as the Bhagavad Gita is included in the *Mahabharata*. Many believe it is a manual for spiritual and moral conduct and see it as one of Hinduism's most significant works.

Arjuna, a warrior prince, and Lord Krishna, his charioteer, converse in the Bhagavad Gita. Arjuna is prepared to lead his army against his own relatives in the struggle for control of the kingdom. When Arjuna recognizes members of his family and friends among the enemy, he is struck with sorrow and uncertainty and loses all motivation to fight.

According to the Bhagavad Gita, Arjuna was overcome with contradictory feelings and skepticism about the rationale for the war on the eve of the War of Kurukshetra. He was considering the possibility of engaging in combat with and killing his own family members and teachers and was debating on how to proceed. Lord Krishna, an incarnation of the Hindu god Vishnu, was Arjuna's charioteer and companion. Arjuna confided his worries and uncertainties to him.

In response, Lord Krishna gave a speech known as the Bhagavad Gita, which contains some of the most profound philosophical ideas. Krishna imparted to Arjuna the nature of the self, the universe, and the divine, as well as yoga's potential for achieving nirvana. Krishna further emphasized that Arjuna's job as a warrior was to battle and carry out his dharma, regardless of the result.

Arjuna was advised by Krishna to execute his deeds as an act of worship rather than becoming emotionally connected to the results of what happened. He emphasized that death was merely a change from one form to another and that the actual self was everlasting and indestructible.

Lord Krishna inspired Arjuna to engage in combat with bravery, tenacity, and objectivity. After overcoming his fears and trepidations, Arjuna bravely took part in the War of Kurukshetra. The Bhagavad Gita has since become one of Hinduism's most revered literary masterpieces, and its message of esoteric wisdom has inspired millions of people all over the world.

Karna

One of the most fascinating narratives in the *Mahabharata* is the tale of Karna's birth. The myth claims that Kunti, the mother of the Pandavas, gave birth to Karna before she wed Pandu.

As the story goes, Kunti was intrigued and anxious to test the power of the boon she was granted by the sage Durvasa. She wanted to try out this ability to summon any god and have a child with them.

Kunti made the decision to test the boon's effectiveness one day. She requested a son from Surya, the sun god, and gave birth to Karna. However, Kunti abandoned the infant Karna in a basket and floated him down a river out of fear that having a child out of wedlock would have negative social repercussions.

Adhiratha and Radha, a childless couple, ultimately discovered the basket and took the infant in as their own. They gave him the name Vasusena. The child grew to become a proficient archer and warrior. Vasusena had a natural knack for weapons, and Dhritarashtra soon learned of his abilities.

Vasusena discovered his true identity when he grew older and realized that he was Karna, Kunti's abandoned son. The news originally devastated him, but he soon made up his mind to prove himself a warrior and win the admiration and respect of his fellow soldiers.

There were difficulties on Karna's path to fame and glory. Due to his humble origins, he experienced prejudice and derision from some quarters, but he was unfazed and devoted to his training. Karna swiftly outperformed many of his contemporaries in terms of his ability to use a bow and arrow, and he became known as a legendary warrior.

Later, during the War of Kurukshetra, Karna turned into a crucial ally of the Kauravas, the Pandavas' cousins. He bravely fought for them, but his allegiance to the Kaurava prince and his companion, Duryodhana, brought about his demise. Karna was ultimately beaten in a brutal battle by Arjuna, one of the Pandava brothers, despite his remarkable bravery and talents.

Death of Karna.
https://commons.wikimedia.org/wiki/File:Death_of_Karna.jpg

The Tale of Drona

Drona was renowned for his prowess as a warrior, mentor, and friend. His deeds and way of life were crucial to the circumstances that set off the War of Kurukshetra.

Drona is the revered teacher for both the Kauravas and the Pandavas throughout the epic. He is a significant counselor and fighter in the narrative. Drona is acknowledged as the son of the sage Bharadvaja, although Drona was not born to a mother. Bharadvaja sees a beautiful apsara (somewhat similar to a nymph) and is overcome with lust. He spills his seed into a pot, giving birth to Drona.

Bharadvaja teaches Drona and Prince Drupada at his hermitage. He teaches the children knowledge of the mystical weapons known as astras and superior military techniques. Drona and Drupada become good friends, and Drona promises to help Drupada for the rest of his life. Eventually, Drupada gains the throne of Panchala, while Drona adopts a simple lifestyle as a wise man and teacher. The chapter also introduces Ashwatthama, Drona's son.

Drona was known for his rigorous teaching methods, and he evaluated his students' loyalty in addition to their skills. He was the one behind shaping Arjuna into a master archer and a committed defender of morality. Arjuna received criticism from other pupils for being given preference, but Drona defended his decision by putting the other students through a loyalty test. Only Arjuna demonstrated everlasting loyalty.

Arjuna was taught the art of fighting by Drona, including how to use the Brahmastra sword. He also taught Prince Duryodhana how to become a proficient warrior and how to destroy Arjuna's brothers, the Pandavas. Drona supported Duryodhana and his army during the War of Kurukshetra. He was an extremely tough opponent, and his proficiency with the Brahmastra, combined with his warrior prowess, made him practically unbeatable.

However, Drona resisted Duryodhana's attempt to use him to murder the Pandavas because he understood that it went against his role as a teacher. A teacher should not injure their own pupils. When Duryodhana detected his reluctance, he deceived Drona into thinking that his son Ashwatthama had been killed in combat. Drona unleashed the Brahmastra in a moment of fury and despair, causing extensive damage and devastation.

Drona was ultimately defeated by the Pandavas in combat through guile and trickery. Both sides lamented his passing since he was so well liked and recognized for his abilities and moral character.

The story of Drona in the *Mahabharata* serves as a warning of the perils of arrogance, retaliation, and mistaken allegiance. It demonstrates how even the most knowledgeable and wise can succumb to their emotions and forget their true calling in life.

Conclusion

The *Mahabharata*, an important ancient Indian epic, describes a dynastic conflict between two branches of a royal dynasty. In addition to providing insight into ancient Indian civilization, it also explores a variety of philosophical and ethical questions.

Hindi, Tamil, Telugu, and Bengali are only a few of the languages in which the epic has been translated. Its characters and tales are still present in Indian popular culture, and they have served as an inspiration for several plays, films, and television shows. The themes of dharma, karma, and *moksha* continue to be important in Hinduism, and its teachings have also influenced Indian philosophy and spirituality.

Chapter 9: Tales from the *Ramayana*

The *Ramayana* is the other important Hindu epic. This Sanskrit epic is largely attributed to Maharishi Valmiki, a legendary poet of his time, who composed it sometime after 300 BCE. The epic consists of over twenty-four thousand shlokas, or couplets, spread out over seven books.

The *Ramayana* follows the life and adventures of Rama during his exile. The epic holds great value in Hindu and Buddhist traditions. Rama's story illustrates what an ideal society ought to look like, from the formation of the state to its people. The narration of history, *itihasa*, is combined with morals and lessons on human life.

Who Were Rama and Sita?

Rama and Sita.
Ayan Gupta, CC BY-SA 3.0 <https://creativecommons.org/licenses/by-sa/3.0>, via Wikimedia Commons; https://commons.wikimedia.org/wiki/File:Ram-Sita.jpg

The protagonist, Rama, is an avatar of the god Vishnu. Rama was the son of Dasharatha, the king of the Kosala Kingdom. After Rama's marriage to Sita, his life was marked by challenges and tribulations that began with his exile from his rightful kingdom. Rama is known to have three brothers: Lakshmana, Bharata, and Shatrughna.

As mentioned, Rama was the incarnation of Vishnu in human form. Vishnu reportedly took on the responsibility of dealing with Ravana, who had spread chaos throughout the world. He took this vow when the demigods turned to Brahma for help against the demon. The texts describe Rama's early life and upbringing as virtuous. Rama was polite and kind and had a reserved personality. He was taught the Vedas, the Vedangas (which aid in the study and understanding of the Vedas), and martial arts.

As well as the female protagonist of the *Ramayana*, Sita was the wife of Rama and is considered the human incarnation of the goddess Lakshmi. She is known as the daughter of the earth goddess Bhumi but was brought up by the king of Videha, Janaka, as his adopted daughter. She is said to have been found in a furrowed field by the king, who took her in and raised her as his own.

Sita and Rama married after Rama won a bow-stringing contest. Sita chose him from a group of eligible suitors. Sita also chose to go to Ayodhya, Rama's birthplace, with him to spend their lives together. She accompanied him in his later exile. Much of the *Ramayana* is focused on Rama's efforts to retrieve Sita when she was taken by Ravana. The epic also features other characters central to the story.

Hanuman

Statue of Hanuman.
MatrixInDWD, CC BY-SA 4.0 <https://creativecommons.org/licenses/by-sa/4.0>, via Wikimedia Commons; https://commons.wikimedia.org/wiki/File:Statue_of_Lord_Hanuman_at_Dharwad.jpg

A central character, Hanuman is a divine ape god appointed to be Rama's companion. In addition to being an avatar of Shiva, Hanuman is regarded as the son of Vayu, the god of the wind. Hanuman is believed to have been born to Anjana and Kesari but is regarded as the spiritual son of Vayu due to the role the wind god played in his birth. He was born as an ape due to a curse placed on his mother by a sage whom she had angered.

According to legend, King Dasharatha was performing a ritual to have children, during which he was given a pudding by the gods to give to his three wives. This pudding allowed his wives to bear sons. Some of this pudding was taken away by a bird. The wind pushed the bird into the outstretched hands of Kesara, who had been praying to be blessed with a child. Hanuman was thus born by the grace of Vayu.

Ravana

Statue of Ravana.
Indi Samarajiva, CC BY 2.0 <https://creativecommons.org/licenses/by/2.0>, via Wikimedia Commons; https://commons.wikimedia.org/wiki/File:Ravana_Statue.jpg

Ravana acts as the antagonist in the *Ramayana*. He is the multi-headed demon-king of Lanka. While a well-learned scholar, Ravana is portrayed as an evil character who spreads strife and kidnaps the wife of Rama. Born to Vishrava and Kaikesi as their eldest son, Ravana is known to be devoted to Shiva. He is often portrayed as having ten heads, although he is sometimes shown with nine; in those tales, he cut off a head in devotion to Shiva.

Ravana's scholarly pursuits include the authorship of *Ravana Samhita*, a book on astrology, and he also was knowledgeable in medicine and politics. He was a master of the veena. Brahma also granted Ravana a boon: the gift of immortality, allowing him invincibility from the hands of all creations of Brahma except humans. Ravana received weapons, a chariot, and the power of shapeshifting from Brahma in response to the sacrifices Ravana made.

Exile to the Forest

After Rama and Sita were married, the two traveled to Ayodhya to spend their lives together. At this time, King Dasharatha, who had been growing old, was considering giving the crown to his eldest son. This proved a popular decision in the court and among his subjects, who all approved of the quiet and kind Rama as their king. But this decision did not sit well with Kaikeyi, the second wife of the king and stepmother to Rama. In Rama's absence, after the king had made the decision of who should ascend his throne, the queen reminded him of his promise that he had made to her a while ago to comply with any one thing that she asked.

The king remembered and was bound by his promise, so he agreed to hear her request. The queen demanded that Rama be exiled to the forest of Dandaka for fourteen years, giving her son, Bharata, enough time to become king and gain the people's favor. This request was not well received by any of the royal family. Even Bharata opposed his mother's request. However, Rama wanted his father to fulfill the promise he had made to his wife, stating that he had no wish for a throne or other material trappings of the earthly world.

Against the wishes of others, including his father and brother, Rama chose to go into exile as his stepmother had requested after discussing the matter with Sita. While Dasharatha grieved at Kaikeyi's request, and even though Bharata asked his brother not to go, he undertook this journey, stating that time passes quickly. As he was leaving, Bharata promised Rama that he would rule the kingdom in his name until he returned. When Rama and Sita left to go into exile, they were followed by Lakshmana, who accompanied Rama out of brotherly love.

The Period of Exile

After Rama and Sita left the Kingdom of Kosala, they spent some time on the banks of the River Mandakini in a region called Chitrakoot, located on the borders of modern-day Madhya Pradesh and Uttar Pradesh. During this time, Rama and Sita stayed with a sage called Vasishtha. Rama also met Shabari, a devotee of his, who offered her own berries to Rama to eat, first testing each one to ensure it was sweet.

The following years of exile passed as Rama and Sita roamed through the forests and lived with various sages, such as Atri. The two lived a quiet and simple life in the wild, offering protection from demons to those being harassed and persecuted and attempting to live humbly without depending on the material comforts of the world. The two lived this way for the next ten years until Ravana turned his attention toward them.

Sita's Abduction

After ten years of exile, Rama and Sita settled on the banks of the River Godavari in a place called Panchavati. This region was plagued by demons, and one such demon brought chaos to Rama's and Sati's lives. Surpanakha, who is said to be the sister of Ravana and might have been sent by him, caught sight of Rama and was infatuated with him. She attempted to seduce him, but her advances were rejected.

Infuriated, Surpanakha threatened Sati, and in response, Lakshmana cut off her nose and ears. These events reached Ravana, who sought revenge on Rama for the treatment of his sister. He tracked Rama and Sati down, but when he laid eyes on Sati, he was enchanted by her beauty and began to hatch a plan to obtain her.

He ordered his servant, Maricha, to disguise himself as a golden deer. This deer was meant to lure Rama and Lakshmana away from Sita. However, Rama and Lakshmana did not forget Sita in their haste. Lakshmana drew a protective circle around Sita, forbidding her to leave it until the two returned. Ravana knew about Sita's kindness, though. He appeared before her as an old beggar, asking for food. In pity, Sita stepped out of the circle, and Ravana was able to grab her, throwing her in his flying chariot. Hearing her screams for help, a passing bird, Jatayu, tried to save her, only to have its wings cut off by Ravana. In the hopes of rescue, Sita threw down her necklace so Rama could find her.

The Defeat of Ravana

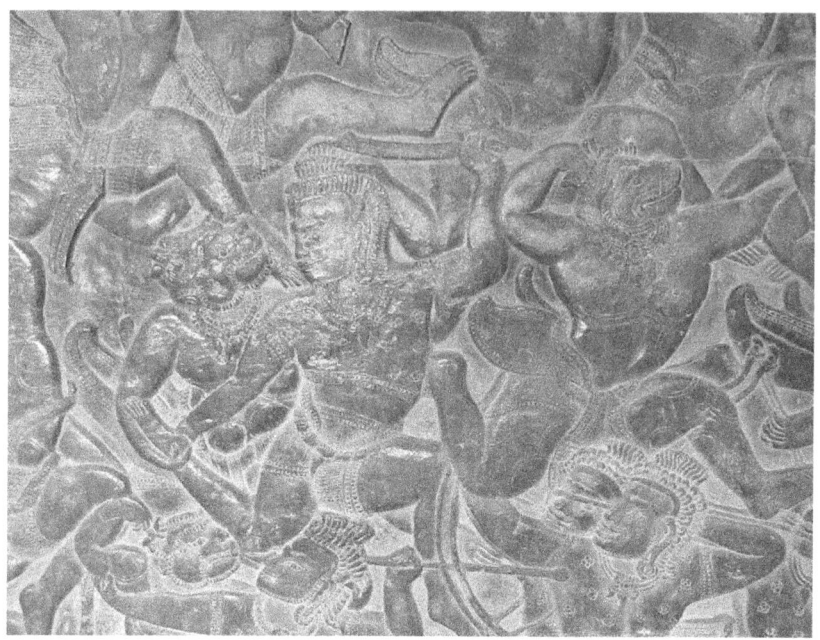

The Battle of Lanka at Angkor Wat.
Photo Dharma from Penang, Malaysia, CC BY 2.0 <https://creativecommons.org/licenses/by/2.0>, via Wikimedia Commons; https://commons.wikimedia.org/wiki/File:Angkor_Wat_-_103_Battle_of_Lanka_(8581635902).jpg

When Rama and Lakshmana returned, they learned of Sita's kidnapping from Jatayu. The two immediately set out in search of Sita, but they despaired since they had no means to travel swiftly and nothing to aid them in their journey. They had no resources to fight Ravana and free Sita. Traveling south, they met the sage Shabari, who led them to Hanuman.

Lakshmana and Rama headed to the Monkey Kingdom of Vanara to meet Hanuman, who was a devotee of Rama and an ape hero. Hanuman was minister to Sugriva, who had been banished from his rightful throne of Kishkindha by his brother Vali. To earn Sugriva's support and trust, Rama and Lakshmana decided to help him by killing Vali and establishing him as the head of his kingdom. In exchange, Sugriva promised to help rescue Sita.

However, Sugriva became enmeshed in his newly regained kingdom and forgot his promises to Rama. Lakshmana was angered at the treachery, and in his rage, he threatened to destroy the ape citadel over which Sugriva reigned. But before this could happen, Tara, the former ape queen and wife of Vali, intervened. She convinced Sugriva to stand by his word.

Thus, search parties were sent out to the north, east, west, and south. Three parties came back bearing no news, having heard nothing of Ravana or Sita. The southern party, led by Angada and Hanuman, learned from a vulture, a brother to Jatayu, that Sita had been taken by Ravana to the land of Lanka, which refers to modern-day Sri Lanka. Ravana had attempted to convince Sita to become his consort, but she repeatedly refused his advances.

Hanuman's Heroics

Armed with the knowledge of Sita's location, Hanuman took the lead, taking on the form of a gargantuan ape and leaping across the sea to Lanka. His journey to Lanka was beset with tests and challenges, including a demon who challenged his abilities and a mountain that offered him rest and comfort. Yet Hanuman proved himself time and time again. When he finally reached Lanka, he was met by the demon Lankini, who was charged with the protection of Lanka.

Lankini had seen the end of Lanka should she fall. Hanuman was able to defeat her, thereby gaining entry into Lanka. Once inside, Hanuman spied on Ravana and was able to track down where Sita was being held. He also witnessed Ravana terrorizing and threatening her in an attempt to convince her to become his wife.

When Ravana and his demon guards left, Hanuman was able to reach out to Sita. He assured her that Rama was still alive, offering his signet ring as proof of her husband's existence. He then offered to carry her back to Rama. Sita refused, stating that such a rescue must be done by Rama in order to avenge her. As proof of her being alive, Sita gave Hanuman her comb to give to Rama.

Before Hanuman left to inform Rama of what had transpired between him and Sita, he chose to create trouble for Ravana. Hanuman wreaked havoc in Lanka by uprooting trees, destroying buildings, and killing many of Ravana's soldiers. In order to meet with Ravana, Hanuman allowed himself to be captured. When he was before Ravana, he demanded that the demon release Sita. In response, Ravana set Hanuman's tail on fire. Hanuman escaped, leaping from roof to roof and setting Ravana's citadel on fire. He then returned to Kishkindha to deliver the news to Rama.

The War between Rama and Ravana

Following Hanuman's return, Rama and Lakshmana began to prepare their armies to march to Lanka. At the shore of the southern sea, they were joined by Ravana's brother, Vibhishana, who sought vengeance against Ravana for throwing him out of the kingdom. As the armies sought to cross the sea, the apes Nila and Nala created a floating bridge made from stones that had Rama's name written on them. These stones were blessed and could not sink. In other narrations, the curse of a sage prevented anything thrown by the two from sinking.

After the armies crossed the sea and entered Lanka, a long war began. Lakshmana was grievously injured by a powerful weapon shot by Ravana's son Indrajit. In response, Hanuman assumed his gigantic ape form again and leaped from Lanka to the Himalayas in search of an herb that could cure Lakshmana. When he was unable to find it, he took the entire mountain and brought it back to Lanka. The war finally came to an end when Rama was able to kill Ravana. He put Vibhishana on the throne.

Rama was finally able to free Sita, and upon their meeting, he assured her that the dishonor of her abduction had been avenged. However, Sita's return was not met with joy by all. Many from Rama's kingdom raised questions about Sita's purity. In response, Rama sent Sita away, telling her to find some other shelter. Seeking to prove her fidelity, Sita asked Lakshmana to build her a pyre. Praying to the god of fire, Agni, Sita walked into the raging fire. Agni appeared from the flames, carrying Sita in his arms, thus proving her purity. Sita was then joyfully reunited with Rama.

Rama's Reign of Ayodhya

Following the end of their exile, Rama and Sita returned to Ayodhya, accompanied by Lakshmana and Hanuman. There, the two were crowned king and queen, yet their days of prosperity were numbered. Despite Sita's proof of her purity by walking through fire, Rama's subjects again questioned her loyalty since she had resided in another man's house. While Rama was furious with the allegations, he was forced to send Sita into exile into the forest while she was pregnant.

Sita would give birth to her twins, Lava and Kusha, while in exile. When the brothers grew up, they engaged in war with the Kingdom of Kosala, defeating the entire army of Ayodhya, as well as Lakshmana, Shatrughna, and Bharata. They even took Hanuman captive. It was not until Rama arrived that the two brothers were defeated and taken back to

Ayodhya, where they attempted to convince the people of Sita's sacrifice. It was only when Sita herself emerged that Rama realized the captured brothers were his own sons.

Sita still faced challenges to her character. Overwhelmed, she declared that the earth should swallow her whole if she was pure, and sure enough, the earth beneath her feet opened up and swallowed her.

The rest of Rama's rule was uneventful. Eventually, he, along with his brothers, left the world. He returned to his true form as Vishnu and was reunited with Sita, who had already taken her true form as Lakshmi.

Conclusion

Indian mythology forms a significant part of the religious belief system in India and continues to impact the cultural practices of many regions in Southeast Asia. In addition to contributing to religious beliefs and practices, it also had a significant impact on art, poetry, drama, and other works of fiction. It has inspired other forms of artistic expression, including unique dance forms, such as Kathak and Bharatnatyam, which incorporate many features of Hindu mythology in their movements. Indian mythology has also inspired traditional music, such as music created with the sitar and tabla.

Hindu mythology has influenced many cultures outside of India. The Indonesian currency, for example, depicts Ganesha, showing the impact of Hinduism on the country's history and culture. Even video games, such as the *Indus Battle Royale*, images of which were played in Times Square in New York City in 2022, depict Ganesha and other aspects of Hindu mythology. There is even a statue of Shiva outside the CERN building in Switzerland.

The concept of Indo-futurism has taken the world by storm. The concept visualizes a futuristic world through science fiction, art, and music where the Indus Valley civilization inhabits another planet rather than going extinct. This idea features many elements from Hindu mythology and spirituality, such as showing Jatayu with phoenix wings. While the concept itself was created to challenge India's colonial history and the Western views of the future, it has become an increasingly common sight in popular culture.

While portraying perhaps the lesser-known aspects of Hindu mythology, this concept attempts to show Indian mythology as the beacon of the future. In essence, Indo-futurism provides a peek into the future through music, art, film, television, science fiction, and even video games and brings light to the mythology that was misplaced in the annals of colonial history.

We hope you enjoyed this introductory look at Indian mythology, and we encourage you to take a look at our bibliography to continue learning about this fascinating aspect of Indian culture.

Here's another book by Enthralling History that you might like

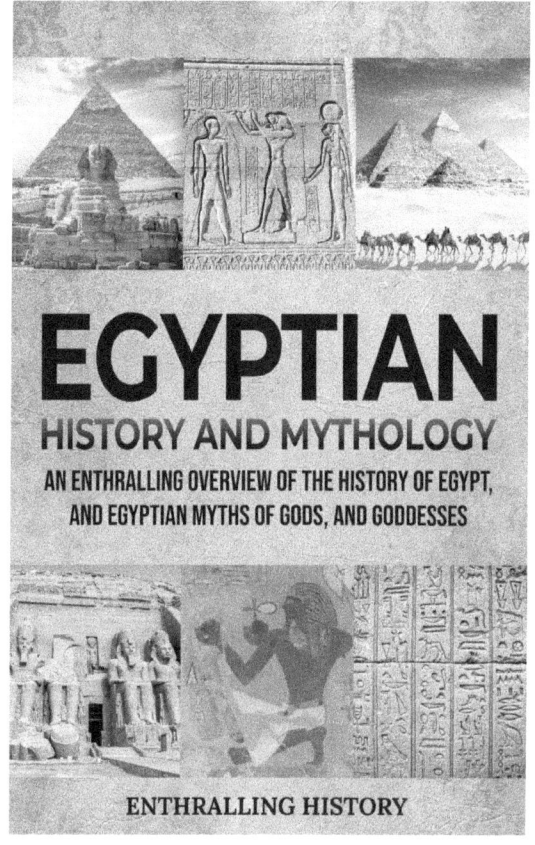

Free limited time bonus

Stop for a moment. We have a free bonus set up for you. The problem is this: we forget 90% of everything that we read after 7 days. Crazy fact, right? Here's the solution: we've created a printable, 1-page pdf summary for this book that you're reading now. All you have to do to get your free pdf summary is to go to the following website:

https://livetolearn.lpages.co/enthrallinghistory/

Once you do, it will be intuitive. Enjoy, and thank you!

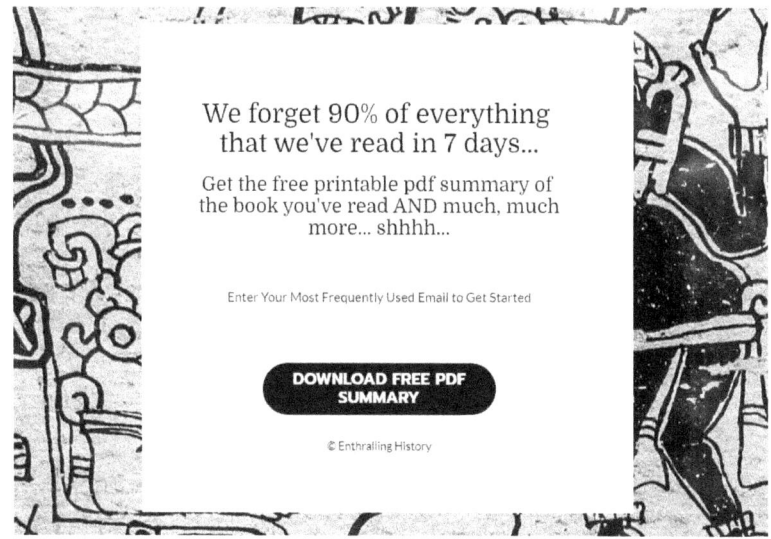

Bibliography

Anon. Rig Veda. Translated Griffith, Ralph TH. 1896.

Babur: tr. Annette Susannah Beveridge. Baburnama, a memoir. 2017 (reprint).

Bharne V & Kruske B. Rediscovering the Hindu Temple. Cambridge Scholars Publishing. 2012.

Chakravarty, Sudeep. Plassey: The Battle That Changed the Course of Indian History. 2020.

Collins, Larry & Lapierre, Dominique. Freedom at Midnight. 1975.

Dalrymple, William. White Mughals. Penguin. 2002.

– Nine Lives. In Search of the Sacred in Modern India. Bloomsbury. 2009.

– The Anarchy: The Relentless Rise of the East India Company. Bloomsbury. 2019.

Eck, Diana. India, a Sacred Geography. 2011.

Eraly, Abraham. The Mughal World. 2007.

Gandhi, Mahatma. Third Class in Indian Railways. 1917.

Godden, Rumer. Gulbadan: Portrait of a Rose Princess at the Mughal Court. 1980.

Herman, Arthur. Gandhi and Churchill: The Epic Rivalry That Destroyed an Empire and Forged Our Age. Random House Digital. 2008.

Michell, George: The Hindu Temple. University of Chicago Press. 1988.

Mukhoty, Ira. Akbar the Great Mughal: A Definitive Biography. 2020.

Nossov, Konstantin. Indian Castles 1206-1526.

Preston, Diana and Michael: A Teardrop on the Cheek of Time. Doubleday. 2007.

Smith, Vincent. Ashoka: The Buddhist Emperor of India. Clarendon Press, Oxford, 1920.

Thapar, Romila. The Penguin History of Early India from the Origins to AD 1300. London 2002.

Tharoor, Shashi. India: From Midnight to the Millennium. 1997.

--- Inglorious Empire: What the British Did to India. 2016.

--- Why I Am a Hindu. 2018.

--- Ambedkar: A life. 2022.

Video

"Sarmada Foundation: Madhubani, a sacred tradition" https://www.youtube.com/watch?v=XO7KPnENbf4&list=WL&index=201&t=1s

Britannica, The Editors of Encyclopedia. "Durga | Goddess, Personality, & Story." *Encyclopedia Britannica*, 2023, https://www.britannica.com/topic/Durga.

Britannica, The Editors of Encyclopedia. "Lakshmi | Hindu deity | Britannica." *Encyclopedia Britannica*, 5 April 2023, https://www.britannica.com/topic/Lakshmi

The British Library. "Princess Sita's Kidnap - The *Ramayana*." *The British Library*

Brown, Norman W. "Theories of Creation in the Rig Veda." *Journal of the American Oriental Society*, vol. 85, no. 1, 1965, pp. 23-25. *JSTOR*, https://doi.org/10.2307/597699.

Burke, Elisabeth. "Vedic Creation Hymn." *Humanities LibreTexts*, 5 May 2021, https://human.libretexts.org/Bookshelves/Religious_Studies/Scriptures_of_the_Worlds_Religions_(Burke)/02%3A_Hindu_Scriptures/2.01%3A_Vedic_Creation_Hymn.

Cartwright, Mark, et al. "Lakshmi." *World History Encyclopedia*, 14 August 2015, https://www.worldhistory.org/Lakshmi/.

Cartwright, Mark, et al. "Saraswati." *World History Encyclopedia*, 25 November 2015, https://www.worldhistory.org/Sarasvati/.

Chandran, Nyshka. "An 'unapologetically Indian' universe." *BBC*, 9 January 2023, https://www.bbc.com/culture/article/20230106-the-ancient-indian-myths-resonating-now.

"CHAPTER IX. THE PURĀNIC ACCOUNT OF THE CREATION." *Hindu Mythology: Vedic and Purānic*, by William Joseph Wilkins, D K Printworld (P) Limited, 2003.

Doniger, Wendy. "Ganesha | Meaning, Symbolism, & Facts | Britannica." *Encyclopedia Britannica*, 1 April 2023, https://www.britannica.com/topic/Ganesha.

Doniger, Wendy. "Parvati, Hindu deity." *Encyclopedia Britannica*, 1 April 2023, https://www.britannica.com/topic/Parvati.

Doniger, Wendy. "Purana | Hindu literature | Britannica." *Encyclopedia Britannica*, 2022, https://www.britannica.com/topic/Purana.

Emory University. "Maa Saraswati | Emory | Michael C. Carlos Museum." *the Carlos Museum*, 2013, https://carlos.emory.edu/maa-saraswati.

"Ganesh and Root Chakra, Lord Ganpati Relation with Muladhara Chakra – Rudraksha Centre." *Rudraksha Ratna*, 2020, https://www.rudraksha-ratna.com/articles/ganesh-the-god-of-root-chakra.

The Goddess Garden. "The Hindu Goddess Parvati." *The Goddess Garden*, 9 November 2018, https://thegoddessgarden.com/the-hindu-goddess-parvati/.

Heaphy, Linda. "The Hindu God Ganesh - Who is this Elephant Headed Fellow Anyway?" *Kashgar*, 2020, https://kashgar.com.au/blogs/gods-goddesses/the-hindu-god-ganesh-who-is-this-elephant-headed-deity-anyway.

HISTORY. "Hinduism - Origins, Facts & Beliefs." *HISTORY*, 2019, https://www.history.com/topics/religion/hinduism.

Liu, H. "Multiverse (Religion)." *Scholarly Community Encyclopedia*, Encyclopedia MDPI, 21 November 2022, https://encyclopedia.pub/entry/35469.

Lotus Sculpture. "Ganesha Hindu God, the Remover Obstacles, Learn About Ganesh." *Lotus Sculpture*, 2022, https://www.lotussculpture.com/ganesha-hindu-god-ganapati-elephant-meaning-symbolism.html.

Marin, Kimi. "Your Base Power: Ganesha and the First Chakra - Beyogi." *beYogi*, 22 June 2015, https://beyogi.com/your-base-power-ganesha-first-chakra/.

Mathur, Priyanshi. "Ganesh Chaturthi 2019: 10 Lesser-Known Short Stories of Bal Ganesha You Need to Know." *Indiatimes.com*, 9 October 2019, https://www.indiatimes.com/trending/social-relevance/ganesh-chaturthi-short-stories-374788.html.

Murphy, Anne. "*Ramayana.*" *Asia Society*, 2020, https://asiasociety.org/education/Ramayana.

New World Encyclopedia. "Parvati." *New World Encyclopedia*, 2023, https://www.newworldencyclopedia.org/entry/Parvati.

Pattanaik, Devdutt. "HT Brunch Cover Story: 5 stories from the *Ramayana* you haven't heard before." *Hindustan Times*, 24 May 2020, https://www.hindustantimes.com/brunch/ht-brunch-cover-story-5-stories-from-the-Ramayana-you-haven-t-heard-before/story-nuCPzKqscCqJZTJAFJiF2K.html

Rajhans, Gyan. "The Goddess Durga: The Mother of the Hindu Universe." *Learn Religions*, 14 January 2019, https://www.learnreligions.com/goddess-durga-1770363.

Sahota, Peter. "Creation in the Rig Veda. One of its several narratives in... | by Peter Sahota | Desire to Think." *Medium*, 23 February 2020, https://medium.com/desiretothink/creation-in-the-rig-veda-8772c3569d20.

Shreemaa. "Story of How Ravana Kidnapped Sita." *Devi Mandir*, 2023, https://www.shreemaa.org/story-how-ravana-kidnapped-sita/.

Singh, Soham. "The Hindu Mythology of India and Its Influence on Eastern Culture." *Gobookmart*, 3 January 2023, https://gobookmart.com/the-hindu-mythology-of-india-and-its-influence-on-eastern-culture/.

Sivananda, Sri Swami. "Ganesha – The Divine Life Society." *The Divine Life Society*, 2020, https://www.dlshq.org/religions/ganesha/.

TemplePurohit. "Ganesha Stories - 7 Most Popular Stories of Ganesha." *TemplePurohit*, 5 March 2022, https://www.templepurohit.com/ganesha-stories-7-popular-stories-of-ganesha/.

Trivedi, Raj. "Folktales from *Ramayana* – Talking Myths." *Talking Myths*, 2020, https://talkingmyths.com/category/folktale/folktales-from-Ramayana/

University of British Columbia. "Vedic Theory of Creation." *UBC Computer Science*, 2006, https://www.cs.ubc.ca/~goyal/creation.php

www.ingramcontent.com/pod-product-compliance
Lightning Source LLC
Chambersburg PA
CBHW070327010526
44107CB00004B/446